ENGLISH GRAMMAR to

ACE

NEW TESTAMENT GREEK

English Grammar to Ace New Testament Greek
Copyright © 2004 by Samuel Lamerson

Requests for information should be addressed to:

Zondervan, *3900 Sparks Dr. SE, Grand Rapids, Michigan 49546*

ISBN 978-0-310-25534-5

Interior design by Pamela J. L. Eicher

Printed in the United States of America

ENGLISH GRAMMAR to

ACE

NEW TESTAMENT GREEK

SAMUEL LAMERSON

ZONDERVAN®

For Cindy, who gave me courage

CONTENTS

ACKNOWLEDGMENTS

A book like this is not written alone. There are a number of people who deserve great thanks. A few are listed below.

Dr. Fowler White and Dr. Ron Kilpatrick from Knox Seminary have both been gracious in giving me time to work on this project and in getting me the books I needed. The friendship of all of the other members of the faculty has been invaluable

My children, Charity and Josiah, have been patient while I worked on "one more example" before we went to the movies. They are gifts from God.

My friend Fred VonKamecke and I have had many talks about the Greek language and how best to teach it. This friendship has benefited me greatly.

This book is better because of the careful editing of Verlyn Verbrugge. He has saved me from many errors. I appreciate Zondervan's being willing to take a chance on a first-time author.

My friend and mentor Scot McKnight has helped me in more ways than he knows. I thank God for Scot's friendship, scholarship, and kindness.

My wife, Cindy, to whom this book is dedicated, has been a wonderful encourager. I could not have completed this project without her. She is a gift from God and is exactly the gift I needed.

Finally, I must thank our Lord for telling us stories in the beautiful Greek language. His story is beautiful in any language but especially so in Greek.

Δόξα ἐν ὑψίστοις θεῷ

INTRODUCTION

WHY THIS BOOK?

In six years of teaching first-year Greek at the seminary level, it has become apparent to me that one of the greatest stumbling blocks to learning a foreign language is the lack of familiarity with the basic grammar of one's mother tongue. It is, after all, difficult to understand how a Greek infinitive differs from an English infinitive if you do not know what an infinitive is. I hope that this book will meet a need among those students who enter the first year of Greek study with fear and trembling.

This book is written for that student who has been out of school for some time and has forgotten a great deal of grammatical knowledge. There may be others who, while they have not been out of school for a great length of time, still need a refresher course on grammatical terms and concepts. Others may have simply "gotten by" in school without ever really getting a grasp of basic grammar. This book is not a substitute for a full English grammar. It is a "quick refresher course" for those who find themselves in need either before or during their Greek studies. If you are in any of these categories, this book is for you.

HOW TO USE THIS BOOK

This book is set up so that it can be used in a variety of ways. For example, the professor can use it as a guide in refreshing the student's English grammar during the first session of each new chapter, assigning the corresponding chapter for the grammatical concept being studied (e.g., for deponent verbs, read ch. 10 in this book).

Or one can also take what I believe is a better approach: to study the entire book for the first few class sessions, and then review the pertinent chapters and exercises as the class moves along in a first-year grammar. It is for this reason that many of the exercises have both Greek and English. One can initially do the exercises in English, then go back for a review when the corresponding chapter is studied in the Greek class. Don't feel bad about not being able to read the Greek exercises at first. By the end of the first year, you will have no trouble with the English or the Greek exercises.

I truly believe that this small tome can be a great help to you as you enter the wonderful world of New Testament Greek. Too often students let unfamiliarity with English grammatical concepts quench the thirst for the study of the Greek language. With this book as a road map, the journey should be much easier.

I have tried to make this book as fun and entertaining as possible. This has not always been easy (after all, it is a book about grammar). I hope it will help you to overcome whatever fear you may have of the study of language and allow a little fun to creep into your study. Because I paid my way through school by working as an entertainer (you may catch a rerun of my juggling act on Nickelodeon), I hope that some of this book will be entertaining as well as informative. The study of Greek can, and should be, a fun, rewarding, and spiritual experience. Don't let any second-year students tell you different.

TIPS FOR STUDYING GREEK (AND ENGLISH)

Here are a few general tips on using this book and on learning New Testament Greek.

1. *Read for understanding.* Make sure that as you read the textbook, you read slowly and carefully

before moving on to the next chapter. Make a serious effort to master the major components of a chapter before continuing.

2. *Work daily.* A course in New Testament Greek might tempt some students to study merely in order to prepare for class, in semi-weekly sessions. A much more productive method of study is to set aside sixty to ninety minutes per day (five to six days per week) to work on Greek. Organize your life to keep the "tyranny of the urgent" from robbing you of an opportunity to learn the language well.

3. *Work hard.* The most important part of learning any language is discipline. There simply is no substitute for the hard work of memorizing, reading, working through the examples, and working hard to try to understand what each lesson is attempting to teach. Above all, keep up with your assignments both in grammar and (especially) in vocabulary. Once you get behind, you need to work doubly hard to catch up as the class moves ahead.

4. *Work smart.* Use the tools that are at hand for you. The computer tools that are available either for your PC or your handheld device are wonderful ways to keep up with your vocabulary. If you are using Mounce's *Basics of Biblical Greek* (*BBG*), you should make use of the CD that comes with the book as well as think about purchasing the vocabulary program for your handheld device.

5. *Learn the proper terminology.* Many times a student's problem stems not from the fact that she cannot understand a particular concept, but from

the fact that she does not understand the terms that are being used. In Appendix 1 of this work you will find a glossary of select grammatical terms. When these terms are used in the body of the text, they will be followed by an asterisk (*) indicating that you may find a short definition of the term in the appendix.

6. *Don't neglect your vocabulary!* This is critical. All the grammatical knowledge in the world will be of little value to you if you do not know what the words mean. In Appendix 2 you will find some suggestions for vocabulary memorization.

1

NOUNS:
You Ain't Nothing but a Noun Dog!

DEVOTIONAL

Mark 5:2–3 When Jesus got out of the boat, a man with an evil spirit came from the tombs to meet him. This man lived in the tombs, and no one could bind him any more, not even with a chain.

καὶ ἐξελθόντος αὐτοῦ ἐκ τοῦ πλοίου εὐθὺς ὑπήντησεν αὐτῷ ἐκ τῶν μνημείων ἄνθρωπος ἐν πνεύματι ἀκαθάρτῳ, ὃς τὴν κατοίκησιν εἶχεν ἐν τοῖς μνήμασιν, καὶ οὐδὲ ἁλύσει οὐκέτι οὐδεὶς ἐδύνατο αὐτὸν δῆσαι.

We have a new resident at our house. He was a gift from the local humane society and his name is "Buddy." Buddy is a large, beautiful golden retriever. The problem is that Buddy seems to have been mistreated by his former owner, which has led to certain eccentric behaviors. He has a great deal of difficulty going through doors (a very serious problem for a dog who needs to go outside); he walks around the house most of the time with all the grace of a pig on ice skates, his feet slipping and sliding with every step. Moreover, he is deathly afraid of thunderstorms—a fact that we discovered when we came home to find the cat door torn off its hinges and resting around Buddy's neck like some sort of a square collar. In short, Buddy can be a nuisance, which is, I am sure, why his former owners gave him away.

The man in today's Scripture reading is just such a nuisance. He doesn't know how to act, he won't wear his clothes, he breaks the chains whenever anyone tries to control him. If there was a "human dog pound," he would be there. Instead, he lives by himself, out in the cemetery where no one cares about him. The amazing thing is that Jesus comes and changes everything. With a few words he delivers the man from the grasp of Satan and gives him his life back. The man puts his clothes back on and sits down, and his life is forever altered for the better.

We have kept Buddy, though I have often been tempted (and, yes, have even threatened) to take him back to the pound. I suppose the reason why I have not taken him back to the pound is because he needs us. And in truth we need him to remind us of what God has done for us. He has taken us into his family, and even though we are fearful and less than graceful, and we even break things, he still loves us.

The message of Christianity is that we all belong in the pound. But we have been adopted into the family of God through the sacrifice of our Lord Jesus Christ. Let us be thankful to God for the ultimate sacrifice of his son, Jesus.

INTRODUCTION

Science fiction author Ray Bradbury, when asked where he comes up with his ideas, refers to his "noun list." He makes lists of nouns and then develops characters, stories, and even novels based on a single noun. You can see that the noun is a very important part of the English language. It is as important, if not more important, in Greek.

DEFINITION

The noun, as you may remember from your elementary English class, is *a person, place, thing, or idea.*

- ☞ person: Abraham, John, Matthew, Moses
- ☞ place: Nazareth, Bethlehem, Galilee
- ☞ thing: sickness, water, hand
- ☞ idea: truth, peace, fear

Nouns, then, can name something that you can touch (a door, a person) or something you can only think about (truth, love). Nouns are the backbone of sentences. They are not what make sentences move along (that would be verbs), but they are what does the moving or are moved along. How then are the English nouns like and not like Greek nouns?

Similarities. In Greek the nouns indicate a person, place, thing, or idea, just as they do in English. There are, however, certain important differences in the nouns of these two languages.

Differences. (1) In English most nouns do not have gender*. That is, most nouns that do not refer to living beings are neither masculine nor feminine. This is not the case in Greek. Every noun is either masculine, feminine, or neuter. This does not indicate anything about the meaning of the noun; rather, it is simply the way that those who spoke the language thought of these words. You will learn to determine the gender of a noun based on the article that is attached to the vocabulary word when you learn it.

(2) A second difference has to do with a noun's function in the sentence. In English we are able to determine the subject generally because it occurs before the verb.

- ☞ John hit the ball. ("John" is the subject; his name occurs before the verb.)

☞   The ball hit John. ("Ball" is the subject; it occurs
      before the verb.)

In Greek, by contrast, we are able to tell what function nouns
play in the sentence not by their place but by the ending that occurs
on the noun. This is what we mean by declension*. Greek, unlike
English, is a highly inflected language. That means that the reader
can tell how a noun functions in a sentence, regardless of where it
occurs, simply by its ending. In Greek, nouns are divided into three
different classes (called *declensions*) and each class has its own
small quirks. There are several important things to remember:

☞   A different declension is simply a different way of
      spelling. It does not affect the meaning of the noun.

☞   All nouns take the same article. That is, despite
      the fact that there are three different declensions
      of endings for nouns, there is only one set of end-
      ings (three genders) for the article. Thus, the arti-
      cle will remain constant despite the change in
      ending of the noun. See chapter 3 on the article.

NAME	MNEMONIC	KEY WORD	ARTICLE
Nominative	This case nominates the subject of the sentence.		ὁ ἡ τό οἱ αἱ τά
Genitive	This case generates a description of the noun.	of	τοῦ τῆς τοῦ τῶν τῶν τῶν
Dative	Two or Four people go on a date. The dative is usually translated using "to" or "for." It tells the indirect object and can usually be recognized by the iota (either subscripted or obvious) in its ending.	to or for	τῷ τῇ τῷ τοῖς ταῖς τοῖς
Accusative	This case accuses the subject of what it is, has, or will do. It will usually answer the question who or what is receiving the action (as opposed to the subject, who is usually doing the action).	sometimes in or by	τόν τήν τό τούς τάς τά
Vocative	This is the case of vocal chords or directly calling someone. It usually looks exactly like the nominative		

EXERCISES

Circle the nouns in the following sentences.

1. The man held the dog on a leash.

2. The Greek book is thicker than I want it to be.

3. The Bible is God's true word.

4. I want to master the Greek language.

5. We all went to the park for an outing.

6. Our lunch was eaten over our homework.

7. Vocabulary is what I should be spending my time on.

8. I love Greek.

9. (Mark 4:8) Still other seed fell on good soil.

    Καὶ ἄλλα ἔπεσεν εἰς τὴν γῆν καλὴν

10. (Revelation 1:6) To him be glory and power for ever and ever! Amen.

    αὐτῷ ἡ δόξα καὶ τὸ κράτος εἰς τοὺς αἰῶνας τῶν αἰώνων· ἀμήν.

11. (Revelation 1:8) "I am the Alpha and the Omega."

    Ἐγώ εἰμι τὸ Ἄλφα καὶ τὸ Ὦ.

12. (Jude 2) Mercy, peace and love be yours in abundance.

    ἔλεος ὑμῖν καὶ εἰρήνη καὶ ἀγάπη πληθυνθείη.

2

INFLECTION:
Trouble Understanding Yoda You Have, Yes?
The Nature of Inflected Languages

DEVOTIONAL

Mark 2:10 But that you may know that the Son of Man has authority on earth to forgive sins. . . ." He said to the paralytic,

ἵνα δὲ εἰδῆτε ὅτι ἐξουσίαν ἔχει ὁ υἱὸς τοῦ ἀνθρώπου ἀφιέναι ἁμαρτίας ἐπὶ τῆς γῆς—λέγει τῷ παραλυτικῷ

In this passage one can become confused if it were not for the fact that the Greek language is inflected. It might be difficult to tell if the paralytic is speaking to someone else or if the Son of Man is speaking to the paralytic. This is the reason that knowing about cases for nouns is so important. One cannot tell the subject from the object without knowing the cases.

Jesus is here healing a man who has been lame for a long time. He has little help and almost no hope for the future, yet when he meets Jesus everything changes. His life will never be the same, and he will never forget that one meeting.

As you go through your first-year of Greek, there will be times when you feel like this man. It will seem as if you cannot help yourself and no one else cares to help you. Always remember that you are not alone. You not only have many students in your class to "pick you up and carry you," but you also have our Lord to whom you can turn. With his help you will be able to get through the difficult times and look back with a realization that those times taught you more that you could ever have imagined.

INTRODUCTION

If you have ever watched the character Yoda in the *Star Wars* movies, you have noticed that he speaks in an unusual manner. He is speaking English, but he is sometimes difficult to understand because of the word order in his sentences. This trouble only happens because Yoda is speaking English. If he were to speak Latin or Greek, the difficulty would be almost nonexistent.

The Greek language uses what are called *inflections*. The same word is spelled slightly differently depending on the way that it functions in a sentence. You can recognize a subject in an English sentence because it usually comes before the verb. You will learn to recognize a subject in Greek because of the way that it is spelled. It makes little difference, in Greek, where the noun occurs in the sentence.

In English our pronouns are inflected (e.g., "I," "me," "mine"), but most of our nouns are not. That is, they are not spelled differently based on their use or function in the sentence. In other words, the nouns usually remain the same despite the fact that they serve different functions in the sentence. One example of a noun changing is the added "...'s" when the noun is possessing something. Notice how the word order makes the following sentences clear.

☞ The student gives the teacher a book. (Student gives; teacher receives.)

☞ The teacher gives the student a book. (Teacher gives; student receives.)

The Greek language allows the student to pick out the subject, verb, and direct object no matter where it might fall in the sentence. Thus, one important difference between Greek and English is the use of "endings for nouns." These endings will become clear at the proper time, but for now, think of Yoda and realize that word order should have been more important to him.

The beginning student should make sure that he or she knows and can recognize the major parts of speech in English. The inflected system of Greek will make no sense to you if you do not realize that different words have different functions (different jobs) in the sentence. Before moving any deeper either in this work or in your study of Greek, you must be able to:

☞ define clearly the major parts of a sentence (subject, direct object, verb, pronoun, etc.).

☞ pick out the subject, direct object, and verb in the exercise sentences.

Here are important definitions for the following exercises (please see the glossary in the appendix if you are having trouble with any of these terms):

Verb: Verbs are words that express action, occurrence, or a state of being. Look for a word that speaks of action or existence.

Subject: To find the subject of a sentence, first find the verb; then use questions such as "who?" or "what?" to find the subject. Ask yourself who or what is doing the action that is being recorded by the verb.

Direct Object: Verbs that denote action often require objects to complete the meaning. To find a direct object, find the subject and the verb; use them to ask the question "to whom?" or "to what?" is the action being directed? This question will help you point to the thing or person in a sentence that is the object of the verb.

Word Order*: Usually in English the subject comes first, then the verb, then the object of the verb. This is not true in Greek, which is highly inflected and thus less dependent on word order. See Appendix 3 on sentence diagramming.

EXERCISES

Circle the verb, underline the subject, and draw a box around the direct object.

1. The student hit the Greek book.

2. The Greek book hit the student.

3. The young student was hit by the old professor.

4. The professor hit the student.

5. The Greek book has a name on the cover.

6. The class enjoyed the Greek professor.

7. John ignored the class assignment.

8. Cynthia answered the questions correctly.

9. The Greek professor frightens the students.

10. The students frighten the Greek professor.

11. (John 1:6) There came a man who was sent from God.
    Ἐγένετο ἄνθρωπος ἀπεσταλμένος παρὰ θεοῦ, ὄνομα αὐτῷ Ἰωάννης.

12. (James 1:5) If any of you lacks wisdom, he should ask God, who gives.

   Εἰ δέ τις ὑμῶν λείπεται σοφίας, αἰτείτω παρὰ τοῦ διδόντος θεοῦ.

13. (Mark 1:13) He was with the wild animals, and angels attended him.

   καὶ ἦν μετὰ τῶν θηρίων, καὶ οἱ ἄγγελοι διηκόνουν αὐτῷ.

14. (1 Corinthians 1:4) I always thank God for you.

   Εὐχαριστῶ τῷ θεῷ μου πάντοτε περὶ ὑμῶν.

15. (Galatians 1:11) The gospel I preached is not something that man made up.

   τὸ εὐαγγέλιον τὸ εὐαγγελισθὲν ὑπ᾿ ἐμοῦ ... οὐκ ἔστιν κατὰ ἄνθρωπον.

3

THE ARTICLE:
The Rosetta Stone of the Greek Language, or The Article Is Your Friend, The Other One Is a Relative

DEVOTIONAL

Titus 2:13 while we wait for the blessed hope—the glorious appearing of our great God and Savior, Jesus Christ

προσδεχόμενοι τὴν μακαρίαν ἐλπίδα καὶ ἐπιφάνειαν τῆς δόξης τοῦ μεγάλου θεοῦ καὶ σωτῆρος ἡμῶν Ἰησοῦ Χριστοῦ

The text of Titus 2:13 speaks of "our great God and Savior, Jesus Christ." Those who wish to deny this clear use of the term "God" in speaking of Jesus indicate (wrongly) that there are two different people being spoken of here. One is the Father, who is called "the great God," and the other is the Son, who is called "Savior, Jesus Christ."

The key to understanding that this passage speaks of one person and not two resides in an understanding of the Greek article. Later on in your Greek studies, you will learn that the use of the article can be one of the most important parts of Greek syntax*. This use of the article is called the "Granville-Sharp Rule," and you will learn about the rule as your facility with the language grows.

For now it is enough to realize that great grammarians have shown that this passage clearly uses the term "God" to speak of Jesus. One can only realize this fact after studying the Greek text. If we believe that Jesus is God and that he has called us to this task, we must do our absolute best in our own work for him. We are studying Greek not for a grade, or a degree, or even a diploma, but for a better knowledge of our great God and Savior.

INTRODUCTION

You might have, when you were a child, sent away for a "decoder ring" (I still have mine) so that you and your friends could send secret messages without anyone knowing what they were. It was all going very well until my sister found my ring. The article is somewhat like the decoder ring or the Rosetta Stone of Greek.

The Rosetta Stone is one of the most important finds in recent history in terms of language translation. This stone was found in a small Egyptian village in 1799. The stone has the same message in three different languages. Thus, this stone enabled linguists (because of their being able to compare one known language with another unknown) to make great strides in understanding and translating ancient languages.

The article is somewhat like that stone. There will be some substantives* (particularly those that follow the pattern of the third declension) that may give you a little trouble as to their gender*, number*, or case*. Always remember that the article, like the Rosetta Stone, is to be compared with the substantive. The article is your friend; don't forget about your friends.

DEFINITION

The definite *article** is the word "the," which precedes a substantive* to specify a definite substantive (rather than an indefinite one). In English there are three categories of articular usage.

The first is the substantive that occurs without the article. This is called an anarthrous* usage. The second is the substantive that occurs with the indefinite article ("a" or "an"). The third is the definite article ("the"). Examples of the three uses are:

- ☞ little red wagon—anarthrous
- ☞ a little red wagon—indefinite article
- ☞ the little red wagon—definite article

Differences. There are two main differences between the English and the Greek article. The first is that in Greek there is no indefinite article. Thus, the substantive will either be anarthrous* or articular*; that is, it will either have a definite article or it will not. Unlike English, which has a middle ground, no such ground exists in Greek.

The second difference is larger and perhaps more important. Like nouns, adjectives, and participles in Greek, the article is highly inflected*. That is, just as there are different cases for a noun, depending on the usage in the sentence, there are different cases for the definite article. Thus, the article becomes the "Rosetta Stone" of the Greek language. One can always tell the gender, number, and case of a substantive based on the article (if the word has an article; remember that a noun might also be anarthrous).

This will be particularly helpful as you begin to learn the somewhat difficult third declension* nouns. The great thing about the article is that, while substantives are spelled differently depending on the part of speech and declension, the article never changes. As a result, the article is your friend. When other substantives forsake you with quirky changes of spelling or morphological difficulties, the article will be the same—a great friend who does not change.

EXERCISES

Circle the definite article and underline the indefinite article. Put a box around any noun that does not have an article (is anarthrous).

1. The book was not very clear.

2. I had an apple for lunch and a salad for supper.

3. A man gave the last speech of the day, a woman the first speech.

4. A boat is not the greatest investment of one's money.

5. Who is the fan who helped cause the Cubs' loss in game six of the series?

6. (John 1:1) In the beginning was the Word, and the Word was with God, and the Word was God.

   Ἐν ἀρχῇ ἦν ὁ λόγος, καὶ ὁ λόγος ἦν πρὸς τὸν θεόν, καὶ θεὸς ἦν ὁ λόγος.

7. (John 1:4) In him was life.

   ἐν αὐτῷ ζωὴ ἦν.

8. (John 1:6) There came a man who was sent from God.

   Ἐγένετο ἄνθρωπος ἀπεσταλμένος παρὰ θεοῦ.

9. (John 1:8) He came only as a witness to the light.

   ἀλλ᾽ ἵνα μαρτυρήσῃ περὶ τοῦ φωτός.

10. (John 1:9) The true light that gives light to every man was coming into the world.

Ἦν τὸ φῶς τὸ ἀληθινόν, ὃ φωτίζει πάντα ἄνθρωπον, ἐρχόμενον εἰς τὸν κόσμον.

ADJECTIVE:
What Color Is an Adjective?
The Carnival Talkers of the Greek World

DEVOTIONAL

Hebrews 13:20 May the God of peace, who through the blood of the eternal covenant brought back from the dead our Lord Jesus, that great Shepherd of the sheep

ὁ δὲ θεὸς τῆς εἰρήνης, ὁ ἀναγαγὼν ἐκ νεκρῶν τὸν ποιμένα τῶν προβάτων τὸν μέγαν ἐν αἵματι διαθήκης αἰωνίου, τὸν κύριον ἡμῶν Ἰησοῦν

There is a danger in our language of the overuse and misuse of some adjectives. The word "literal" occurs far too frequently and is beginning to lose its value. Perhaps the most egregious error is the use of the word "great." There are great TV shows, great meals at fast food restaurants, great lawnmowers, and the greatest show on earth!

The New Testament's use of the adjective "great" is far more constrained. When an author uses the word great, it usually means something that is extraordinary. We find a use of the adjective "great" (*mega*) in Hebrews 13:20. It is strange in some sense because it modifies the noun "shepherd." You may know that during the time of Christ and for some time after, shepherds were not looked upon with any sense of greatness. It was a job held by those who were often considered untrustworthy. Yet the writer to the Hebrews considers Christ as our "great Shepherd."

Jesus has taken the metaphor of the shepherd and redefined it. During the time of David, being a shepherd was a wonderful vocation. This vocation had dropped in public opinion since that time. Jesus urges us to think back to that time and remember that he is the shepherd who gave his life for his sheep.

Those of you who are studying for the ministry will also one day be shepherds. While the adjective "great" will certainly not be applied to you in the same sense that it was of Christ, you may still be a "great shepherd"—one who loves his sheep and always wants what is best for them. If the shepherd does not take care of his sheep, who will?

INTRODUCTION

If you have ever had the privilege of attending what is called a "ten in one show" at a carnival, you will remember that there was a person (almost always a man) standing outside the show talking about what wonders you would see inside. He was describing the girl who would change into a gorilla, the magician's wonders, and many other things that sounded as though they simply could not be missed.

This man's job is that of the "talker"; he stands outside and "pitches" the show to those walking by, hoping that with his description he will be able to convince some to pay the entrance fee in order that they can see the wonders that await inside. If you have ever attended one of these shows, you may have been surprised to see that the "talker" sometimes was one of the acts as well. He "stood in" as a substitute for an act after having described the act outside the tent.

The adjective is the carnival talker of the Greek world. It will describe the wonders of the substantives* and sometimes, just like the "talker," stand in for the noun as a substantive*. These adjectives are fascinating, so get ready to go into the tent and see the "world's greatest Greek words: Alive! Alive! Alive!"

DEFINITION

An *adjective* is a word that describes a substantive*. Examples would be "the *red* car," "the *good* book," or "the *great* game." Thus, an adjective tells the reader something about the noun or substantive; it is a word of description. One of the questions that one might ask to determine whether or not a word is an adjective is: "Does this word give me more information about the substantive?" If it does, it is likely an adjective.

Similarities. There are two things that link the English and the Greek adjective together. Both describe (as pointed out above) and both can be used "substantively*." That is, adjectives can be used as nouns. Think of the phrase "out with the bad and in with the good." Both "bad" and "good" are adjectives but are used substantively in this sentence. A more familiar example, using these same words, would be "the good, the bad, and the ugly." In usual phrases the terms "good, bad, and ugly" would be followed by a noun: a *good* book, a *bad* card, or an *ugly* set of notes. In this case, however, the adjective stands in place of the noun. It is substituting for the noun (thus the term *substantive*). I tell my students to think of the substantive as the substitute teacher of the Greek world—not quite the same as the regular teacher, but still trying to get the job done.

Differences. While there are similarities between the adjectives in both languages, there are also some fairly large differences. The most significant difference is that the adjective in Greek is highly inflected*. This means that any adjective can be either masculine, feminine, or neuter as well as any of the cases that we have learned in chapters 1 and 2.

The fact that the adjectives are inflected leads to another difference. Adjectives will match the noun that they refer to in gender*, number*, and case*. This can often be a helpful grammatical aid. An example might be the sentence, "The boy caught the dog while he was howling." The question, of course, that comes to mind is to which noun does the adjective "howling" (actually, a verbal adjective, technically called a participle) refer? Was the boy howling because he could not catch the dog, or was the dog howling because he was caught? This problem would, for the most part, be solved in Greek.

While it is sometimes difficult to determine the particular use of an adjective, what follows are three simple questions that may help you in your efforts to find the exact use of a particular Greek adjective:

1.   Is there a noun that the adjective is modifying? If not, then it must be substantival; if so, then it must be adjectival.

2.   Does the adjective have an article? If so, then it must be attributive* (this use will become clear to you as you study the chapter on adjectives in your Greek grammar); if not, then it could be either attributive or predicate.

3.   Does the context of the sentence seem to demand the verb "to be" but the verb is not there? If so, then an anarthrous* adjective is likely predicate*; otherwise, it is attributive.

CONCLUSION

Don't forget to think of the adjective as the "carnival talker" of the grammatical world. It is the part of speech that tells us about the wonderful, horrible, beautiful, or terrible things that wait inside the "noun tent." Don't overlook the wonderful work of these delightful words.

EXERCISES

Circle the adjectives and draw an arrow to the noun or pronoun that the adjective is modifying. If there is no noun (i.e., the adjective is substantival), place an asterisk beside the circle.

1. Josiah was tired of carrying the heavy Greek grammar.

2. The Greek professor, like the carnival hypnotist, had the ability to put the students into a deep sleep.

3. Nathan loved the good and hated the bad.

4. The light was red, but the driver drove through in spite of this fact.

5. In magic there are many different kinds of card tricks.

6. (Revelation 3:15) I know your deeds, that you are neither cold nor hot.

   οἶδά σου τὰ ἔργα ὅτι οὔτε ψυχρὸς εἶ οὔτε ζεστός.

7. (Mark 7:27) It is not right [or good] to take the children's bread and toss it to their dogs.

   οὐ γάρ ἐστιν καλὸν λαβεῖν τὸν ἄρτον τῶν τέκνων καὶ τοῖς κυναρίοις βαλεῖν.

8. (Matthew 6:23) But if your eyes are bad, your whole body will be full of darkness.

   ἐὰν δὲ ὁ ὀφθαλμός σου πονηρὸς ᾖ, ὅλον τὸ σῶμά σου σκοτεινὸν ἔσται.

9. (Matthew 6:14) For if you forgive men when they sin against you, your heavenly Father will also forgive you.

   Ἐὰν γὰρ ἀφῆτε τοῖς ἀνθρώποις τὰ παραπτώματα αὐτῶν, ἀφήσει καὶ ὑμῖν ὁ πατὴρ ὑμῶν ὁ οὐράνιος.

10. (Matthew 6:13) And lead us not into temptation, but deliver us from the evil one.

    καὶ μὴ εἰσενέγκῃς ἡμᾶς εἰς πειρασμόν, ἀλλὰ ῥῦσαι ἡμᾶς ἀπὸ τοῦ πονηροῦ.

Note: When you learn more about reading adjectives in Greek, you will learn that there is a question about the translation of this last verse. Some versions translate it "... deliver us from evil." Others (like the NIV above) translate it as "... deliver us from the evil one." This has to do with the use of the adjective, and it is just one of the many wonderful pieces of information that the learning of Greek will open up to you.

5

PRONOUN:
A Noun That Has Lost Its Amateur Status

DEVOTIONAL

Luke 22:70 They all asked, "Are you then the Son of God?" He replied, "You are right in saying I am."

εἶπαν δὲ πάντες, Σὺ οὖν εἶ ὁ υἱὸς τοῦ θεοῦ; ὁ δὲ πρὸς αὐτοὺς ἔφη, Ὑμεῖς λέγετε ὅτι ἐγώ εἰμι.

You will notice that this quotation is from the trial of Christ before the chief priests. He is asked a specific question about his own identity. He answers the question as to his identity as the Son of God by saying: "I am." There are several important things that one should notice about the use of the pronouns in this sentence.

The first is that this saying "I am" is the same as the saying used by God when asked by Moses about his name. It seems likely that Jesus was expecting these Jewish rulers to know and remember this. To answer a question about one's own deity with these words was (in the minds of his accusers) to pile blasphemy upon blasphemy.

The second point that one should see is not readily apparent in the English text. You will learn that in Greek, the subject of the verb is contained (in pronoun form) inside the verb itself. Please do not understand this to mean that the pronoun is literally contained (i.e., you can see it in there) but that it is hiding inside the form of the verb.

The point is that because the verb has no need for the pronoun, when a pronoun is used with a Greek verb, it is done for emphasis. When Jesus answers this question, he not only uses the verb (εἰμί) but also the pronoun (ἐγώ), indicating that he wants the hearers to understand that he is emphasizing, almost underlining, his answer. He is the Son of God and has made that claim clearly here.

This is one reason why we study the Greek language. You only discover this nuance by knowing how Greek works. No matter how good a translation is, there is no substitute for actually being able to read another language. These wonderful things that we see will be paying off for a lifetime—the time that you spend studying your Greek.

INTRODUCTION

When you think of a professional athlete, you think of someone who has become a player for money. That is, this person is no longer a high school player or a college player; he or she now plays for a different reason, for a living. The money has taken the place of the other things that used to be the motivations for the game.

The pronoun is not a professional athlete, but there are some similarities. The pronoun takes the place of a noun in the same way that the money now stands in place of the other motivations for the professional athlete. Always remember that the pronoun has come in off the bench to take the place of the regular noun, perhaps to give it a rest or perhaps because the noun has become injured. The pronoun may be second string, but it is just glad to be in the sentence.

DEFINITION

The pronoun takes the place of a noun. We use pronouns every day in order to make both our writing and our speaking easier. We say, "John went to the store so that *he* could get some milk," rather than, "John went to the store so that John could get some milk." In the first sentence we understand that John is the person who went to the store as well as the one who went to get the milk. In order to save time and monotonous redundancy, we use the pronoun.

There are three persons of pronouns, and these three are the same three persons that you will learn about when we study the verb. If you look ahead at the chart in the next chapter, you will see that there are only three persons and that each person can have either a singular or a plural manifestation.

Similarities. Both in English and in Greek the pronouns are strange. They are both highly inflected. As a matter of fact, the pronoun in English is one of the most highly inflected parts of speech in our language. It is one of the few places where one can, without the appealing to the context, see the difference between the nominative ("I"), the genitive ("my, mine"), the dative ("to me"), and the accusative ("me").

Differences. The most difficult thing about Greek pronouns is that the inflections are strange. The nominative in the first person has very little physical resemblance to the genitive. This will be troublesome for some but a small mnemonic may help. Remember that the second person pronoun is "you." The mnemonic help is to realize that the plural of the second person in Greek will always begin with the letter "u" (an upsilon [υ]). Thus, "u" should make you think of "you."

EXERCISES

Circle any and all pronouns in the following sentences.

1. The girl went out for a walk with her dog.

2. Charity was beautiful but was also kind.

3. Cindy took the Greek book and threw it into a lake in her back yard.

4. I think that throwing the Greek book was harsh, but she thought that it was important.

5. Do you think you would ever throw your Greek book?

6. (Matthew 5:1) He went up on a mountainside and sat down.

   ἀνέβη εἰς τὸ ὄρος· καὶ καθίσαντος αὐτοῦ.

7. (Matthew 5:14) You are the light of the world.

   Ὑμεῖς ἐστε τὸ φῶς τοῦ κόσμου.

8. (Matthew 5:16) Let your light shine before men, that they may see your good deeds and praise your Father in heaven.

   λαμψάτω τὸ φῶς ὑμῶν ἔμπροσθεν τῶν ἀνθρώπων, ὅπως ἴδωσιν ὑμῶν τὰ καλὰ ἔργα καὶ δοξάσωσιν τὸν πατέρα ὑμῶν τὸν ἐν τοῖς οὐρανοῖς.

9. (Matthew 5:27) You have heard that it was said

   Ἠκούσατε ὅτι ἐρρέθη.

10. (Matthew 7:20) Thus, by their fruit you will recognize them.

    ἄρα γε ἀπὸ τῶν καρπῶν αὐτῶν ἐπιγνώσεσθε αὐτούς.

6

VERBS:
Verbs Have Things to Do

DEVOTIONAL

Mark 4:37 A furious squall came up, and the waves broke over the boat, so that it was nearly swamped.

καὶ γίνεται λαῖλαψ μεγάλη ἀνέμου, καὶ τὰ κύματα ἐπέβαλλεν εἰς τὸ πλοῖον, ὥστε ἤδη γεμίζεσθαι τὸ πλοῖον.

"He took the wind out of my sails." Have you ever wondered where this saying comes from? In nonmotorized boat races, a boater can come up behind you with his large sail and catch all the wind before it arrives in your sail. Thus, he slows you down by taking "the wind out of your sails." This saying is so misunderstood today that it often appears as "the wind out of my sales." This totally misses the metaphor.

A metaphor that you will be more familiar with is that of being "swamped." This may become all too familiar to you as you study this year. The saying also has nautical beginnings. It comes from the idea of a boat being filled up with water by large waves and thus sinking.

This term is used in Mark 4:37 to speak of a boat in a storm. The Greek word used is *epeballen* (ἐπέβαλλεν), a verb in the imperfect* tense*. This verb tense here indicates that the waves did not just crash over the boat once, but kept on crashing over the boat with such regularity that the disciples were afraid that they might drown. Thus the tense of this verb, which is difficult if not impossible to see in English translation, indicates an ongoing action in the past, not just a one-time occurrence. The disciples were bailing for their very lives.

By way of contrast, one should not miss the action in which the Lord is engaged in this story. While the disciples are wildly bailing out the boat, he is asleep in the stern. This is the only story in the entire the New Testament where we find Jesus sleeping. Mark teaches us here that when we find ourselves "swamped" by the difficulties of life and our boat ready to go under, we should turn to the Lord, who can sleep under the most difficult of circumstances. When the waves beat time and time again against you and you are in danger of being swamped, turn to the Lord. If he can sleep in the midst of the storm, you should be able to as well.

DEFINITIONS

While most of the definitions are found in the glossary at the back of the book, it is important that a few terms be understood before we move into our overview of verbs.

Person. Every finite verb (see below for a definition of a finite verb) can be first, second, or third person. In the first person, you are speaking of yourself; in the second person, you are speaking to someone else; in the third person, you are speaking about someone or something else to another (a third) person. These are the only three possibilities for the person of a verb.

Number. Every verb form will also have a number. Don't confuse this with person (even though the person is first, second, or third). The number is only one of two possibilities: singular or plural. It should be noted here that in classical Greek there is a "dual," which means a pair (of hands, eyes, or legs). This "dual" occurs in Hebrew as well, but it does not occur in New Testament Greek. The plural of a first-person verb changes from "I" to "we," and so on. The following chart helps to explain these two concepts of person and number, along with some mnemonic aids.

Number	Translation	Reason
First	I	One person present
Second	you	Two people present
Third	he, she, it, or proper noun	Three items present

Mood. This is the most difficult concept for the English-speaking student. Suffice it to say that, in simple terms, the mood indicates the verb's relation to reality. Thus, a verb indicating that something has happened is in a different mood from that indicating that something might happen.

Finite verb. A finite verb is any verb that has a person. For example, you will learn that an infinitive* or a participle* does not have person (e.g., they are not first-person singular) and therefore they are not finite verbs.

DIFFERENCES BETWEEN GREEK AND ENGLISH VERBS

One of the most significant differences between Greek and English verbs is that in Greek, the subject* of the verb can be contained inside the verb itself. Thus, one word in Greek can be an entire sentence. For example, the Greek word *legō* (λέγω) means "I am saying" or "I say." This takes at least two words in English, but only one word in Greek. This may take a little getting used to, but once you understand the concept of person, you will see that the person of the verb is included in the verb itself, not outside as in English.

This is not to say that the person may not be further explained by a noun outside of the verb. For example, the verb *legei* (λέγει) means "he says." If the writer wanted to give the reader an explanation as to who the "he" was, the sentence would read *legei Bubba* (λέγει Βυββα), which would mean "Bubba says." I am not sure that there was anyone named "Bubba" in Israel, but there might have been in the southern part.

The following chart should help in asking the proper questions and thus in making the correct decisions as to the tense*, voice*, mood*, person*, number*, and source*.

Verbal Parsing Chart

Ask yourself these questions:

Tense: How does the speaker view the time/kind of action?	Present: The action is continuous.	Future: The action is expected to take place in the future.	Aorist: The action is undefined as to time.
Voice: Who is doing the action?	Active: The subject is doing the action.	Middle: The subject is acting on itself	Passive: The subject is being acted upon.
Mood: How does the speaker view the action in relation to reality?	Indicative: The mood of certainty.	Subjunctive: The mood of possibility. "might"	
Person: Who is doing the action?	First Person: I ... we	Second Person: you ... you	Third Person: he/she/it ... they
Number: How many are doing the action?	Singular	Plural	
Source: What is the source (lexical form) of this verb?			

EXERCISES

Give the person and number for the following verbs and draw a circle around the subject of the verb.

1. He fell asleep in Greek class only to have nightmares about persons and numbers.

2. Charity was the best Greek student in the class.

3. I am reading a little, thin Greek grammar at a big, fat Greek wedding.

4. You must read this book carefully, otherwise you may miss the jokes.

5. If you are having a great time in Greek class, this book will put an end to that.

6. The best Greek student is one who studies vocabulary as well as grammar.

7. Do you understand this chapter about the verbs?

8. Gracie loves the Greek class but is otherwise normal.

9. (Mark 5:1) They went across the lake to the region of the Gerasenes.

    Καὶ ἦλθον εἰς τὸ πέραν τῆς θαλάσσης εἰς τὴν χώραν τῶν Γερασηνῶν.

10. (Mark 5:2) When Jesus got out of the boat, a man with an evil spirit came from the tombs to meet him.

    καὶ ἐξελθόντος αὐτοῦ ἐκ τοῦ πλοίου εὐθὺς ὑπήντησεν

αὐτῷ ἐκ τῶν μνημείων ἄνθρωπος ἐν πνεύματι
ἀκαθάρτῳ.

11. (Mark 5:3) This man lived in the tombs, and no one could
bind him any more, not even with a chain.

ὃς τὴν κατοίκησιν εἶχεν ἐν τοῖς μνήμασιν· καὶ οὐδὲ
ἁλύσει οὐκέτι οὐδεὶς ἐδύνατο αὐτὸν δῆσαι.

12. (Mark 5:4) For he had often been chained hand and foot,
but he tore the chains apart and broke the irons on his
feet. No one was strong enough to subdue him.

διὰ τὸ αὐτὸν πολλάκις πέδαις καὶ ἁλύσεσιν δεδέσθαι
καὶ διεσπάσθαι ὑπ᾽ αὐτοῦ τὰς ἁλύσεις καὶ τὰς πέδας
συντετρῖφθαι, καὶ οὐδεὶς ἴσχυεν αὐτὸν δαμάσαι.

13. (Mark 5:5) Night and day among the tombs and in the hills
he would cry out and cut himself with stones.

καὶ διὰ παντὸς νυκτὸς καὶ ἡμέρας ἐν τοῖς μνήμασιν
καὶ ἐν τοῖς ὄρεσιν ἦν κράζων καὶ κατακόπτων ἑαυτὸν
λίθοις.

14. (Mark 5:6) When he saw Jesus from a distance, he ran and
fell on his knees in front of him.

καὶ ἰδὼν τὸν Ἰησοῦν ἀπὸ μακρόθεν ἔδραμεν καὶ
προσεκύνησεν αὐτῷ.

7

PRESENT:
Keep Reading This:
The Present Tense

DEVOTIONAL

1 John 2:9 Anyone who claims to be in the light but hates his brother is still in the darkness.

ὁ λέγων ἐν τῷ φωτὶ εἶναι καὶ τὸν ἀδελφὸν αὐτοῦ μισῶν ἐν τῇ σκοτίᾳ ἐστὶν ἕως ἄρτι.

This verse may give you a start at first. On the initial reading it seems to be teaching some form of sinless perfection, yet John tells us that his purpose in writing the book is to give the reader assurance (1 John 5:13). How are we to reconcile the assurance offered to us by John with the seeming call for perfection?

The answer lies in the use of the present tense. As you will learn, the present tense* in the indicative* mood* usually indicates an ongoing action. John intends to teach the reader that if one's life is characterized by continuous sin, then one should look carefully at the reality of the conversion experience. It is not one sin but the life of sin that should cause us to wonder about our own lives in Christ.

DEFINITION

The present tense is a verb that, at least in many cases, indicates an action that is taking place at the time of the writing or speaking. In English it is often accompanied by a form of the verb "to be" in order to make the present nature of the verb clear. For example, "John is studying Greek." In Greek there is no need for a form of the verb "to be" to denote continuous action.

Similarities. The Greek present tense is much like the English present tense in many ways. In the indicative mood it usually indicates an action that is ongoing at the present time. In English this is generally indicated in sentences such as "I am learning vocabulary" or "I am reading the book." While this is not the only use of the present tense in the indicative, it is a fine place to begin your understanding of this particular verbal form.

Differences. The differences have to do with the mood* of the verb. Most Greek scholars today believe that the present tense refers to the present time *only* in the indicative*, and that this does not occur 100 percent of the time. In English when one says, "I am rowing the boat," it almost always indicates a present action. Sentences such as "I might row the boat" (in the subjunctive*) or "If need be, I will row the boat" (conditional) do not indicate that the action is taking place at the present time despite the present tense of the verb. Here, context is your good friend.

EXERCISES

Circle the present tense (if it occurs) in the following sentences.

1. The boy was chasing the dog.

2. The Cubs are winning the playoffs.

3. Swim faster!

4. I will be going now.

5. I am studying as hard as I can.

6. (1 John 1:4) We write this to make our joy complete.

   καὶ ταῦτα γράφομεν ἡμεῖς, ἵνα ἡ χαρὰ ἡμῶν ᾖ
   πεπληρωμένη.

7. (James 1:5) If any of you lacks wisdom, he should ask
   God, who gives [just don't consider this a reason for not
   studying].

   Εἰ δέ τις ὑμῶν λείπεται σοφίας, αἰτείτω παρὰ τοῦ
   διδόντος θεοῦ.

8. (James 1:12) Blessed is the man who perseveres under
   trial.

   Μακάριος ἀνὴρ ὃς ὑπομένει πειρασμόν.

9. (James 1:19) Everyone should be quick to listen, slow to
   speak and slow to become angry.

   ἔστω δὲ πᾶς ἄνθρωπος ταχὺς εἰς τὸ ἀκοῦσαι, βραδὺς
   εἰς τὸ λαλῆσαι, βραδὺς εἰς ὀργήν.

10. (James 2:6) But you have insulted the poor.

    ὑμεῖς δὲ ἠτιμάσατε τὸν πτωχόν.

8

CONTRACTION:
Contract Verbs Kill No One

DEVOTIONAL

John 21:15 When they had finished eating, Jesus said to Simon Peter, "Simon son of John, do you truly love me more than these?" "Yes, Lord," he said, "you know that I love you." Jesus said, "Feed my lambs."

Ὅτε οὖν ἠρίστησαν λέγει τῷ Σίμωνι Πέτρῳ ὁ Ἰησοῦς, Σίμων Ἰωάννου, ἀγαπᾷς με πλέον τούτων; λέγει αὐτῷ, Ναί, κύριε, σὺ οἶδας ὅτι φιλῶ σε. λέγει αὐτῷ, Βόσκε τὰ ἀρνία μου.

If you have been around the church for any length of time, chances are you have heard one or more sermons on the difference between God's love for us and our love for God. Often these sermons take as their text John 21, where Jesus is speaking to Peter and asks him the question, "Do you love me more than these?" The speaker will often point out that the word that Peter uses to answer Jesus' question is a different one from the word that Jesus used in the query. This difference is often asked to bear a great deal more weight than is possible. One must always be care-ful when the difference between the two words (particularly syn-onyms) becomes the most important point of the entire passage.

One must realize that words and particularly synonyms have overlapping meaning, depending on the context. If you were asked about the difference between a trunk and a suitcase, you might say that they are basically the same thing. In certain contexts, there might be a difference, but for the most part the meaning of the words overlaps. The same is true of these Greek words that have the meaning "love." It is almost certainly wrong to build an exeget-ical case (especially in John's Gospel, because he is so fond of syn-onyms) based on the difference between two overlapping words.

For our purposes it is important to note several things. First, Peter does say that he loves Christ, and that is the point of the nar-rative. Peter has fallen, but he can now return to his walk with the Lord. All Christians fall, but God, in his graciousness, picks us up and sets us on the road to the celestial city again.

Second, as an exegetical practice, the context is always much more important than the difference (usually very small) between synonyms.

Third, both of these words for love are contract verbs. In our society there are different meanings for the term contract. One of those meanings, when connected with the word "killer," denotes a person who kills others for money. I want to assure you that while contract verbs can be difficult, they will not kill you. Most of you will not even be maimed!

Jesus asks Peter if he loves him. If you love God and his Word, you must be prepared to work hard to understand it. It may be difficult, tiring, and sometimes even (Oh no!) boring, but you must be willing to "play the scales" before you will be able to impro-vise jazz.

DEFINITION

Contract verbs are those verbs whose stem ends in an alpha, epsilon, or omicron. You will learn, when you begin to study verbs, that most Greek verbs have stems that end in a consonant. This consonant is connected to the verbal ending by a connecting vowel. Because the contract verb's stem ends in a vowel rather than a consonant, two vowels come together. When these two vowels are placed side by side, they will "contract" or get together to form a new vowel. This "new" connecting vowel is the only thing that changes in the contract verb. All the other endings that you know remain the same.

Similarities. One of the things that makes contract verbs so difficult is that there is nothing quite like them in the English language. We do not have contract verbs in our tongue, and thus we must make a special effort to understand what is happening to the Greek verb here.

Differences. Because of the two vowels coming together, the main difference that you will see is that the connecting vowels seem to change drastically in use. Think of the two vowels in the contract verbs as boxers. Both want to win and become the connecting vowel, but there (usually) can be only one. Thus they have to "fight it out" for the honor of being the connecting vowel. There are a number of ways that you, the judge of the fight, can tell who wins.

First, you may (but probably will not) want to learn the chart that appears in many first-year textbooks. This chart has a huge number of possibilities and will show the student which vowel wins under any circumstances (think of it as sort of a "fight card").

A second way to judge the fight is to learn the five rules that Mounce gives in his textbook (see pp. 140–42). This is much easier than using the complete chart and will allow you to make the proper judgment in virtually every situation.

Third, a simple mnemonic may be of some help. While this mnemonic will not solve all the contract problems, it will help with a great many of them. Think of the "e" class vowels as "easy." They almost always lose the fight. Think of the "a" class vowels as "aggressive." They win over the easy vowels but sometimes lose in other cases. Think of the "o" class vowels as "overcomers." They are very rarely beaten in the fight. While this mnemonic will not always work, it is a good rule of thumb in dealing with the fight under difficult circumstances.

GOOD NEWS

The good news about these contract verbs is that you are not being asked to compose Greek. While your teacher may have you do a few compositions just to make sure that you understand the concept, your primary goal will be to recognize the verbs after the fight rather than judge who won. This recognition is much easier than judging, and if you work hard for a couple of hours, you will be able to recognize most contracts without any trouble. Don't worry, the contract is not for your life!

EXERCISES

Because there is nothing quite like the contract verb in English, there are no exercises in this chapter. You should note that in spoken English there are things similar to contract verbs. We say things like "I'm gonna knock you if you don't quit bothering me." While the contractions ("I'm" and "don't") are allowable in good printed English, the word "gonna" for "going to" is a slang word that is unacceptable.

PASSIVE VERBS:
They Don't Just Sit There

DEVOTIONAL

Matthew 5:4 Blessed are those who mourn, for they shall be comforted.

μακάριοι οἱ πενθοῦντες, ὅτι αὐτοὶ παρακληθήσονται.

In his most famous sermon, Jesus gives hope to those who are facing serious difficulties. You should note, however, that Jesus does not say who will be doing the comforting or giving the hope. The reason for this is a theological construction used often in Matthew called the *divine passive**. It is obvious from the context that Jesus means to imply that God will comfort those who are mourning. Why then does he not say this outright? Why does he use the passive rather than the active voice of the verb?

The answer lies in the commandment that the follower of Israel's God should not take the name of that God in vain. During the period that scholars call "Second Temple Judaism," the fear of taking God's name in vain was much greater than it is today. Rather than saying outright "God will comfort them," this grammatical construction was used to be sure that God's name was not misused, though it was implied.

We can all learn a lesson from the care that was used to speak of God and the seriousness with which his name was kept holy. One hears the name of God used today with alarming frequency and with disturbing carelessness. When this happens, think back to this Greek construction—a time when not taking God's name in vain even changed the grammar of sentences!

DEFINITION

An active verb is one in which the subject is acting ("Jesus lifted up his eyes") while a passive verb is one in which the subject is receiving the action ("the Son of Man was lifted up"). A simple question will help you decide the "voice*" of a verb: "Is the subject acting or being acted on?" If the subject is acting, then the verb is active. If the subject is passively being acted on, then the verb is passive.

There is little difference between the English passive and the Greek passive. In both cases you will find the subject being acted on, and this will act as a "flashing sign" to remind you that the verb is in the passive voice.

One small clue that will help in picking out the passive voice is that often, in sentences where there is a passive verb, it is followed by a prepositional phrase. This phrase will, in many cases, tell the reader who or what is actually doing the action (since the subject is not acting). Keep this in mind as you look for passive verbs.

EXERCISES

Circle the passive verbs.

1. I went to the store where my foot was run over by a cart that was driven by an elderly lady.

2. Greek is no longer killing me.

3. The man was bitten by the dog after he ran out of the yard.

4. That book must be returned to the library.

5. A tornado hit our house and we were lifted into the land of Miami.

6. (Matthew 7:19) Every tree that does not bear good fruit is cut down and thrown into the fire.

   πᾶν δένδρον μὴ ποιοῦν καρπὸν καλὸν ἐκκόπτεται καὶ εἰς πῦρ βάλλεται.

7. (Matthew 10:29) Are not two sparrows sold for a penny?

   οὐχὶ δύο στρουθία ἀσσαρίου πωλεῖται;

8. (Matthew 11:5) The blind receive sight, the lame walk, those who have leprosy are cured, the deaf hear, the dead are raised, and the good news is preached to the poor.

   τυφλοὶ ἀναβλέπουσιν καὶ χωλοὶ περιπατοῦσιν, λεπροὶ καθαρίζονται καὶ κωφοὶ ἀκούουσιν, καὶ νεκροὶ ἐγείρονται καὶ πτωχοὶ εὐαγγελίζονται.

9. (Acts 10:18) They called out, asking if Simon who was known as Peter was staying there.

καὶ φωνήσαντες ἐπυνθάνοντο εἰ Σίμων ὁ ἐπικαλούμενος Πέτρος ἐνθάδε ξενίζεται.

10. (Romans 1:8) ... because your faith is being reported all over the world.

ὅτι ἡ πίστις ὑμῶν καταγγέλλεται ἐν ὅλῳ τῷ κόσμῳ.

10

DEPONENTS:
Verbs That Have a Memory Problem

DEVOTIONAL

1 Corinthians 2:14 The man without the Spirit does not accept the things that come from the Spirit of God, for they are foolishness to him, and he cannot understand them, because they are spiritually discerned.

ψυχικὸς δὲ ἄνθρωπος οὐ δέχεται τὰ τοῦ πνεύματος τοῦ θεοῦ, μωρία γὰρ αὐτῷ ἐστιν, καὶ οὐ δύναται γνῶναι, ὅτι πνευματικῶς ἀνακρίνεται.

The apostle Paul is making a statement here that flies in the face of much of the wisdom that the Corinthian population had understood. He is pointing out that all true wisdom comes from the Spirit and not from ourselves. It was common during this period to hire teachers who would share with the student the "true mysteries" of the world. Paul turns this idea on its head and says that one cannot get wisdom by seeking for it, but that one must be visited by the Spirit of God, who is the giver of true wisdom.

Paul seems to be telling us why certain people simply cannot understand the simplicity of the gospel. He points out that prior to a visit from God, all the truth of Scripture appears as foolishness.

Thus, the most important (not the only, but the most important) weapon that any evangelist or apologist has is prayer. Apart from a visitation by the Spirit, the best of arguments will fail and the best of evangelistic approaches will be for nothing. All the world is black until the Spirit takes off our blinders and allows us to see the majesty of God's redemptive plan.

After you have been studying Greek for a while, you will notice that the word translated "accept" (the Greek word δέχεται) looks like it should be in the middle/passive* voice. The strange thing is that it is translated not as a passive verb but as an active one. This is because the verb is a deponent, a verb with a memory problem. Because it cannot remember the active form it once had, the middle/passive form is translated as an active.

INTRODUCTION

We have all heard stories of a person who wakes up from a head injury and does not know who he is. Try as he might, he cannot remember his name, his address, his family, or much of anything that happened before the accident. It may be helpful for you to think of deponent verbs as verbs that have been in such an accident. As a result of the accident they cannot remember what their active form was and so must go on, making the best of the situation after the accident. It is for this reason that deponent verbs look like they are middle or passive, but they are translated active. They have "forgotten" their active form.

DEFINITION

In the simplest of terms, a deponent verb is a verb that is middle or passive in form but active in meaning. One can only tell if a verb is deponent by looking at the lexical form* (the vocabulary form given to you in your first-year grammar). If the lexical form for any tense stem (or principal part) is in the middle or passive, then the verb is deponent for that form.

Similarities. One of the difficulties of this element for students is that there is nothing quite like the deponent in the English language. Many students will struggle with this because they simply have no English "hook" to hang the deponent hat on. If you think of the verbs as having a memory problem, this may help to overcome this difficulty.

Helpful mnemonic aid. You will notice that most of the verbs that are deponent end, in their lexical form, with the letters "-ομαι." You will learn, if you have not already, that this ending is pronounced "oh my." Whenever you come across a vocabulary word that ends in "ομαι," you should think to yourself, "Oh my, that is deponent."

EXERCISES

If you have learned to read the Greek alphabet, you will be able to complete this exercise; otherwise, wait until such time as you have learned to read the alphabet.

Circle any of the following verbs that are deponent. What follows is the lexical form* of the verb.

1. παραγίνομαι

2. γίνομαι

3. βάλλω

4. προευαγγελίζομαι

5. δέχομαι

6. λέγω

7. χαρίζομαι

8. ἀρνέομαι

9. λύω

10. πορεύομαι

11

FUTURE:
When Are You Going to Read This?

DEVOTIONAL

Matthew 1:21 "You are to give him the name Jesus, because he will save his people from their sins."

καλέσεις τὸ ὄνομα αὐτοῦ Ἰησοῦν, αὐτὸς γὰρ σώσει τὸν λαὸν αὐτοῦ ἀπὸ τῶν ἁμαρτιῶν αὐτῶν.

In Matthew 1:21 Joseph is commanded to call the name of Mary's future son Jesus. The future tense is used here in an imperatival sense ("you shall call his name Jesus"). When one realizes that there are at least twenty people with the name Jesus in the works of the Jewish historian Josephus, it becomes clear that the name "Jesus" was not nearly as uncommon a name in the Second Temple period as it is today.

Yet the angel does not stop by telling Joseph what the name should be. He follows the future tense with a causal clause: "You shall call His name Jesus, *for* he will save His people from their sins" (NASB). Thus the angel is saying that this Jesus (named after the great Joshua of the Hebrew Bible) is to be different from the many others who have this name. He is different because he will offer true redemption, which is available only through him.

DEFINITION

The future tense is, in general, a tense that points forward to something that will or likely will happen in the future. There are several types of uses of this tense. Most are simply a prediction about what will happen. Some, however, are commands, such as the one that we have seen in the devotional. This is called the imperatival use of the future. Another use is the conditional future*. This is usually indicated by the term *if*: If x happens, then y will happen in the future. Thus the happening is conditioned on whatever action is in the first part of the sentence. For example, your teacher may say to you, "If you do well on the tests, you will receive a good grade." The clause about your grade is conditioned on the performance on the tests.

Similarities. The Greek future is similar to the English future. Both point forward to an action that will take place but has not occurred yet. Both have the possibility of being used as an imperatival form. Who of us has not been told at some time by our mother: "You will be home by ten o'clock!" This is a future tense, yet is used as a command.

Differences. In English, the future tense is usually indicated by the helping verb "will" or "shall." Thus your mother says to you, "You will clean up your room today," or the Greek teacher says, "You shall study your vocabulary."

In Greek there are two differences that the student should keep in mind in the future tense. First, unlike in English, there is no use of the helping verb. Second, the sign of the future tense is indicated by the Greek letter sigma (the sound of "s") added to the verb stem. It may help in memorization to think that the future tense is translated by the term "shall," and "shall" starts with an "s." Therefore, the Greeks have done English speakers a great favor by using the letter sigma to indicate the future tense.

EXERCISES

Circle the future tense and draw a square around the helping verb in each of the following sentences.

1. The boy was called Harry because he was born with a beard. His mother had stated that the prophet said, "He shall be a bearded one." His mother was tickled to death.

2. If the Cubs win this series, they will go on in the playoffs.

3. At the gnome's birthday party, his girlfriend will jump out of a cupcake.

4. Reading this book will put anyone to sleep. One's dreams will be of fat sigmas and skinny deltas.

5. The one who does well in this class shall be the leader of the Greek club in school.

6. (Mark 13:2) Not one stone here will be left on another; every one will be thrown down.

    οὐ μὴ ἀφεθῇ ὧδε λίθος ἐπὶ λίθον ὃς οὐ μὴ καταλυθῇ.

7. (Mark 13:22) For false Christs and false prophets will appear.

    ἐγερθήσονται γὰρ ψευδόχριστοι καὶ ψευδοπροφῆται.

8. (Mark 13:25) The stars will fall from the sky.

    οἱ ἀστέρες ἔσονται ἐκ τοῦ οὐρανοῦ πίπτοντες.

9. (Mark 13:27) And he will send his angels.

    καὶ τότε ἀποστελεῖ τοὺς ἀγγέλους.

10. (Mark 13:30) This generation will certainly not pass away until all these things have happened.

    οὐ μὴ παρέλθῃ ἡ γενεὰ αὕτη μέχρις οὗ ταῦτα πάντα γένηται.

12

VERBS AGAIN:
Principal Parts and the
Art of Motorcycle Maintenance

DEVOTIONAL

Matthew 8:17 "This was to fulfill what was spoken through the prophet Isaiah: 'He took up our infirmities and carried our diseases.'"

ὅπως πληρωθῇ τὸ ῥηθὲν Ἡσαΐου τοῦ προφήτου λέγοντος, Αὐτὸς τὰς ἀσθενείας ἡμῶν ἔλαβεν καὶ τὰς νόσους ἐβάστασεν.

In this passage, Matthew is quoting Isaiah 53:4. The word that is translated "took up" (ἔλαβεν) comes from the Greek word λαμβάνω, which means "to take, receive." Because the Greek word is an aorist tense, it is difficult to make a connection between the original form of the word (in the present tense) and the form that now stands in the text. This is where the study of principal parts is important. Only by understanding and learning the principal parts of a verb can you to make this connection.

Matthew is reminding us in this passage that Christ has taken our sins and infirmities on himself. This should not be taken to mean that we will never have sickness or pain in this life. It should encourage us, however, to realize that a day will come when these pains will no longer exist. Perhaps you are feeling pain at this moment. It may be physical pain, emotional pain, or spiritual pain. Whatever the pain, let me assure you that a day is coming when that pain will be no more. We long for that day, but we also thank our great God and Savior for his work on our behalf.

INTRODUCTION

What is the proper grammatical construction: "The man was hanged," or The man was hung"? To answer the question one needs to look up the word "hang" in the dictionary and find out the past tense form of the verb "to hang." What you are really looking up is the "past tense principal part" of the verb. This is exactly (in reverse actually) what we are doing in Greek when we are asked to recognize principal parts*.

If you have ever owned a motorcycle, or even a bike, you know that while it is all one piece, it is made up of a variety of different components. There are wheels, a chain, handlebars, foot pegs, and many other parts. To change the look of the cycle, one only has to change one of the many parts, but to actually change the nature of the cycle (e.g., from a motorcycle to a car) one needs to change the main or principal part, the body. The same is true of language.

In your Greek book, you will find a list of what most grammars call "principal parts" (Mounce has chosen to call them "tense stems"). There are several things to remember about these tense stems or principal parts.

1. *Each verb has six potential principal parts* (present, future, aorist active, perfect active, perfect middle or passive, and aorist passive). I use the word "potential" because not every form of every verb occurs in the New Testament. In a verb system where

the particular principal part does not occur, most grammars will simply note this with a blank line.

2. *Each principal part has certain verbal forms that can be built off of it.* Just as with a motorcycle you can change the look or feel by changing the wheels or handlebars, the present principal part can be changed to form the imperfect tense, or the present middle, or the present passive. Other changes, however, are more significant; like changing from a motorcycle to a car, no amount of tinkering or small changes will ever make that possible. Trying to form the aorist verb from the present principal part is the same thing. One must not just make small changes, but change the entire principal part. Fortunately for us, the parts are all listed.

3. *Most principal parts are regular* (there are small changes that are explained in most grammars, and most completely in the footnotes in Mounce). Your job (should you choose to accept it) is to *recognize* what verb, in its present tense form, any other principal part comes from. For most verbs this will be easy. You may even think that it is the same bike with just a new front tire. For some verbs there will be some difficulty, and for a few it will be impossible without rote memory. The most difficult of the principal parts have been underlined by Mounce to alert you to their difficulty (see pp. 385–95). I am sorry about some of the irregularities, but I did not invent the language.

4. *The first question that you must ask when faced with a new verb is: "What is the present tense form of that verb?"* For example, if you see the verb ἔλαβον, you simply must know that it is the aorist form of the verb λαμβάνω. There is no way to simplify the procedure.

5. It is for this reason that *unusual principal parts* (e.g., the underlined principal parts in Mounce's list) *must be learned well enough to be recognized.*

A helpful analogy was suggested to me by a friend and fellow Greek teacher, Fred VonKamecke. Think of the verbs as trees. Now think of the verbs with very irregular principal parts as two trees that have grown together in a tangled mess. That is, two verbs have somehow become so entangled that they now only form one verb, with one of the verbs taking over some of the principal parts and the other verb taking over the other principal parts. You should be able to see in your mind that what has happened is that one "tree-verb" has somehow become entangled with another "tree-verb." As a result of this entanglement, one verb has lost the present principal part (having been taken over by the entangling tree) while the other may have lost some other principal parts. Thus, the Greek word for speak (λέγω) is not nearly as difficult if you realize that it has become tangled up with the verb εἴρω—a verb that does not exist in the present tense because the verb λέγω has choked out the present. An example of this kind of thing happening in English is seen in the verb "to be." The present ("be") comes from the Old English verb "beon," whereas the past ("was") comes from the Old English word "waes," the past tense of "wesan." The reason why this verb is so difficult is that it comes from different verbal roots.

EXERCISE

Place the following verbs into the future and past tense.

1. Swim

2. Drive

3. Hit

4. Wrap

5. Eat

6. Go

7. Read

8. Study

9. Follow

10. Bring

13

AORIST:
You Have Already Read This Chapter, Haven't You?

DEVOTIONAL

John 15:6   If anyone does not remain in me, he is like a branch that is thrown away and withers; such branches are picked up, thrown into the fire and burned.

ἐὰν μή τις μένῃ ἐν ἐμοί, ἐβλήθη ἔξω ὡς τὸ κλῆμα καὶ ἐξηράνθη καὶ συνάγουσιν αὐτὰ καὶ εἰς τὸ πῦρ βάλλουσιν καὶ καίεται.

One of the interesting things about John 15:6 is that it contains an aorist* verb* in the indicative* mood*, yet that verb refers to the future tense. As you will find out in this chapter, many of the aorists in the indicative refer to a one-time action, mostly in the past. This is not an inviolable rule, however, as action in this verse refers to something that will happen in the future.

The point that John is making here seems to be that the action (the judgment of God) is so sure that it is as though it has already happened. We live in a society in which it is not popular to speak of the judgment of God. Yet John has no hesitation in telling us to make sure that our salvation is real, because the judgment of God is so sure that it is as though it has already happened.

DESCRIPTION

In Greek, the aorist tense* often shows a past action. In order to form the aorist tense, things get added to the verb—at the end, and (in the indicative*) at the beginning as well.

Similarities. In English we show that a word is in the past tense in one of two ways. For many verbs, we add an "ed" to the end of the verb; these are called strong verbs because they are strong enough to retain their core word (e.g., "turn" becomes "turned" or "open" becomes "opened"). The addition of an epsilon to the beginning of a Greek verb (in the indicative) is called the "augment*," and it acts sort of like the "ed" at the end of English words.

Some English words, however, do not add an "ed" but change the word more significantly. For example, think of "run," which becomes "ran," or "ride," which becomes "rode." These are weak verbs in English and have an equivalent in Greek called the "second aorist." In the second aorist the stem changes rather than just adding something to the beginning and end of the word.

Differences. As has already been mentioned, the aorist adds letters not just to the end of the word as in English but also to the start of the word. This augment will only occur in two tenses in Greek (aorist and imperfect) and in one mood (indicative), so recognizing the augment will narrow down your choices as to what kind of a verb it is.

One of the difficulties beginning students often have is with the dramatic change in some Greek verbs (see the previous chapter on principal parts*). This happens because of two factors: Either the present tense has added some letters, making the student think that these letters should be in the word at all times, or two different verb stems have become joined together in one verb system (see the tree illustration in the principal parts chapter).

One should not think that the aorist is always in the past tense. There are some scholars who argue that the tense is simply the default and has little or no exegetical bearing on the passage. It is best, however (depending, of course, on what your teacher says), to begin by thinking of the aorist as usually speaking of the past tense in the indicative.

EXERCISES

Circle any past tense verbs.

1. The boy hit the ball.

2. The student hit the wall.

3. The quiz is hard.

4. The test was harder.

5. The textbook makes these concepts very clear.

6. (1 Corinthians 15:3a) For what I received I passed on to you as of first importance.

   παρέδωκα γὰρ ὑμῖν ἐν πρώτοις, ὃ καὶ παρέλαβον.

7. (1 Corinthians 15:3b) Christ died for our sins according to the Scriptures.

   Χριστὸς ἀπέθανεν ὑπὲρ τῶν ἁμαρτιῶν ἡμῶν κατὰ τὰς γραφάς.

8. (1 Corinthians 15:5) He appeared to Peter, and then to the Twelve.

   ὤφθη Κηφᾷ, εἶτα τοῖς δώδεκα.

9. (1 Corinthians 15:32) I fought wild beasts in Ephesus.

    ἐθηριομάχησα ἐν Ἐφέσῳ.

10. (Matthew 1:24) When Joseph woke up, he ... took Mary home as his wife.

    ἐγερθεὶς δὲ ὁ Ἰωσὴφ παρέλαβεν τὴν γυναῖκα αὐτοῦ.

14

PERFECT:
That Which Is Perfect Has Come
(But It Is Not This Chapter).

DEVOTIONAL

John 19:30 When he had received the drink, Jesus said, "It is finished." With that, he bowed his head and gave up his spirit.

ὅτε οὖν ἔλαβεν τὸ ὄξος ὁ Ἰησοῦς εἶπεν, Τετέλεσται, καὶ κλίνας τὴν κεφαλὴν παρέδωκεν τὸ πνεῦμα.

The word Τετέλεσται is perhaps the most well-known Greek word in evangelicalism, for it is an integral part of the well-known witnessing program, *Evangelism Explosion*. Jesus is speaking from the cross, and this is the last of his "seven words," which he speaks shortly before he dies.

This word is in the perfect tense, which means that the action it refers to is finished but the results of the action continue on. An example of a Greek word in the perfect tense that has made its way into the English language is εὕρηκα (found in Rev. 3:2). This is the famous word for "I found it" that has essentially come across unchanged into our language as "Eureka." It means that the person has found the answer to a particular problem, and that the finding of this answer will have implications long after the actual finding is over.

In the case of the word from Christ, the theological implications are clear. Christ has finished the atonement on the cross; thus the action is over. Yet one of the greatest of all truths is that this atonement, while having been finished two thousand years ago, has continuing implications. We are saved because the action was finished, the debt was paid, and the sin was covered over. Yet each day our own lives are affected by this word because we continue to be forgiven because of the action that took place so long ago. Thus the action is perfect because it was finished, yet the results continue on long after the action.

DEFINITION

Similarities. In English the perfect tense is formed by using some form of the helping verb "to have" plus the past participle. It indicates a completed action with results that continue into the time of the speaker or writer. Note that the results may continue beyond the time of the speaker or writer, but they at least continue until this time. For example, "The man *has eaten*, therefore he is no longer hungry." This indicates that the man has finished eating (a competed action) and that the results of this action continue on into the time of the writing (he is now, at the time of the writing, no longer hungry). Both the Greek and the English perfect tenses indicate this same form of action.

Differences. One of the main differences between the English and the Greek perfect tenses is that the Greek tense needs no helping verb. The English will always use some form of the helping verb "to have" while the Greek perfect stands alone (or, stated otherwise, contains the helping verb within itself). This difference can lead to some difficulty in translation from the Greek to the

English. While unbreakable rules are hard to come by in first-year language study, you should try, as much as possible, to use some form of the verb "have" when translating the perfect tense.

This will not always be possible and can easily lead to inelegant phrasing. In English translations of the New Testament, one is rarely able to pick out the perfect tenses based on the translation. This places the burden on the exegete to make sure that the nuances of the perfect tense are brought out.

You should note that in English there are three different forms of the perfect tense: the present perfect ("I have seen the Greek book"); the past perfect ("I had seen the Greek book"); and the future perfect ("I will have seen the Greek book"). Most of the time the Greek perfect will fit with the English present perfect tense.

EXERCISES

Circle the perfect verbs (the entire verbal form that is more than one word) in the following sentences.

1. The girl has been driving fast, therefore she received the ticket.

2. Because we have saved our money, we will have a house with a pool.

3. I have loved the Greek class, causing many of my classmates to question my mental stability.

4. We have heard that Greek is an easy class, and our experiences have proven this to be true.

5. She has followed the rule of studying Greek every day and is getting an "A" in the class.

6. (Luke 8:48) Then he said to her, "Daughter, your faith has healed you. Go in peace."

   ὁ δὲ εἶπεν αὐτῇ, Θυγάτηρ, ἡ πίστις σου σέσωκέν σε· πορεύου εἰς εἰρήνην.

7. (Luke 9:36) When the voice had spoken, they found that Jesus was alone. The disciples kept this to themselves, and told no one at that time what they had seen.

   Καὶ ἐν τῷ γενέσθαι τὴν φωνὴν εὑρέθη Ἰησοῦς μόνος. καὶ αὐτοὶ ἐσίγησαν καὶ οὐδενὶ ἀπήγγειλαν ἐν ἐκείναις ταῖς ἡμέραις οὐδὲν ὧν ἑώρακαν.

8. (Luke 10:9) Heal the sick who are there and tell them, 'The kingdom of God is near you.'

   Καὶ θεραπεύετε τοὺς ἐν αὐτῇ ἀσθενεῖς καὶ λέγετε αὐτοῖς, Ἤγγικεν ἐφ᾽ ὑμᾶς ἡ βασελεία τοῦ θεοῦ.

9. (Philippians 3:12) Not that I have already obtained all this, or have already been made perfect, but I press on to take hold of that for which Christ Jesus took hold of me.

   Οὐχ ὅτι ἤδη ἔλαβον ἢ ἤδη τετελείωμαι, διώκω δὲ εἰ καὶ καταλάβω, ἐφ᾽ ᾧ καὶ κατελήμφθην ὑπὸ Χριστοῦ Ἰησοῦ.

10. (Colossians 2:1) I want you to know how much I am struggling for you and for those at Laodicea, and for all who have not met me personally.

    θέλω γὰρ ὑμᾶς εἰδέναι ἡλίκον ἀγῶνα ἔχω ὑπὲρ ὑμῶν καὶ τῶν ἐν Λαοδικείᾳ καὶ ὅσοι οὐχ ἑόρακαν τὸ πρόσωπόν μου ἐν σαρκί.

15

PARTICIPLES:
The Fiji Mermaid of the Greek World, or Why Adverbial Participles Don't Wear a Watch

DEVOTIONAL

James 5:14 Is any one among you sick? He should call for the elders of the church, and the elders should pray over him, anointing him with oil in the name of the Lord.

ἀσθενεῖ τις ἐν ὑμῖν, προσκαλεσάσθω τοὺς πρεσβυτέρους τῆς ἐκκλησίας, καὶ προσευξάσθωσαν ἐπ᾽ αὐτὸν ἀλείψαντες αὐτὸν ἐλαίῳ ἐν τῷ ὀνόματι τοῦ κυρίου.

There are some verbs that are more important than others. Just as in life there is a hierarchy of authority, such a hierarchy exists in grammar. The finite verb* is the controlling verb of the sentence. The participle is given its time and use in comparison with the main verb.

There is some controversy surrounding the anointing with oil in this passage. There are those who see it as semi-sacramental, an outward evidence of God's inward work. There are others who argue that the use of oil in Second Temple Judaism was medicinal.

They point out that in the parable of the good Samaritan the medicinal use of oil is clear. The beaten man has his wounds bound up and oil is poured on them.

In the passage translated above, it is important that the student note (later on when she becomes more familiar with the Greek verbal system) that the finite verb is not the anointing with oil (which has caused such discussion), but the praying. Thus, James is telling us that, whatever we think of the anointing with oil, the more important action is the prayer. We must never think that some sort of "magic" adheres to certain actions, but that the actions are symbol-laden ways of showing what God is doing and has done.

INTRODUCTION

P. T. Barnum is known even today as perhaps the greatest showman ever to have lived. One of his greatest publicity stunts was known as the "Fiji Mermaid." It was billed as having once been a live mermaid, captured off the coast of the Fiji islands. Visitors were treated to glimpse at a small mummified body that was half human and half fish, just as a mermaid would have been expected to look. Closer examination revealed that the "mermaid" was nothing more than half of a shaved monkey sewn to the lower body of a fish and mummified. Thus, the mermaid was nothing more than a cleverly constructed hoax, proving Barnum's most famous saying, "There is a sucker born every minute."

The Greek participle is much like the Fiji mermaid. It is half an adjective and half a verb "sewn" together in some sort of strange form. It is only by realizing that the participle can take the attributes of both a verb and an adjective that the participle can be fully understood. From some angles, the word looks more like a verb, but from other angles, it looks more like an adjective. Thus, it is the "Fiji mermaid" of the Greek world.

DEFINITION

A participle is a verbal adjective. As such it can function both as a verb and as an adjective. Because participles get their time from the main verb, you can think of participles as verbs that "do not wear a watch." They are constantly having to ask for the time from the finite verb. Just as those friends of yours who don't wear a watch are always asking, "What time is it?" the participle is always asking the main verb about the time.

FUNCTIONS

The participle can have two functions both in Greek and in English. First, it can help to explain the verb. This is called the "adverbial participle." In this case the participle helps the reader understand something about the main verb. It could be the time ("I ate *while watching* TV"). It could be the cause ("*Being hungry*, I ate"). Whatever the case, the adverbial participle will always give information relative to the main verb.

The second type of participle, called the adjectival participle, will do one of two things. It will either tell the reader something about a noun in the sentence ("the *running* man . . ."), or it will stand in place of the noun as a substitute (this is called a "gerund" in English and is a place where English grammar differs from Greek in terms of nomenclature). An example of a substantive would be "hate the *running*, but love the *standing*."

THE FORM OF THE PARTICIPLE

There are several things that the beginning student will do well to keep in mind as he or she studies the Greek participle. The first is that the endings are the same as the adjectives you will learn; thus, by the time that you get to participles, you will already know the endings.

The second is that in the New Testament, the article will often appear with the participle. This is one of the things that will help you in distinguishing between a finite verb and a participle because a finite verb will not take the article. Remember that the "article is your friend."

In distinguishing between adverbial and adjectival participles, always use the three questions laid out above in the chapter on adjectives (ch. 4). If these questions are asked carefully and answered correctly, the student will arrive at the proper answer as to what kind of a participle occurs in the phrase or sentence.

Helpful hint on form. Keep in mind that there are (for the most part) only three different tenses of participles in the Greek New Testament: the present, the aorist, and the perfect.

EXERCISES

Note that, for ease of use, the difference between an English participle and a gerund has been overlooked. Circle the participles in the following sentences.

1. The thieving student was kicked out of school.

2. The sleeping girl missed the entire lecture.

3. The guilt was shown by the running one.

4. Because I was feeling sleepy, I missed class.

5. Shocked by the news of 9/11, we sat glued to our TV sets.

6. The burning stove caught the house on fire.

7. Being a Greek teacher, I am heartless.

8. The boy fell after he was running.

9. Before speaking, the man was craving water.

10. The student missed class because his car was not running.

In the following passages, the words that are Greek participles are underlined in the English translation. Please tell what kind of participle this is (of the three noted above).

11. (Luke 1:19) And the angel answering said unto him, I am Gabriel, that stand in the presence of God; and am sent to speak unto thee, and to show thee these good tidings. (KJV)

    καὶ ἀποκριθεὶς ὁ ἄγγελος εἶπεν αὐτῷ, Ἐγώ εἰμι Γαβριὴλ ὁ παρεστηκὼς ἐνώπιον τοῦ θεοῦ, καὶ ἀπεστάλην λαλῆσαι πρὸς σὲ καὶ εὐαγγελίσασθαί σοι ταῦτα.

12. (Luke 2:18) And all they that heard it wondered at those things which were told them by the shepherds. (KJV)

    καὶ πάντες οἱ ἀκούσαντες ἐθαύμασαν περὶ τῶν λαληθέντων ὑπὸ τῶν ποιμένων πρὸς αὐτούς.

13. (Luke 3:16) John answered, saying unto them all, "I indeed baptize you with water." (KJV)

    ἀπεκρίνατο λέγων πᾶσιν ὁ Ἰωάννης, Ἐγὼ μὲν ὕδατι βαπτίζω ὑμᾶς.

14. (Luke 4:40) When the sun was setting, the people brought to Jesus all who had various kinds of sickness, and laying his hands on each one, he healed them.

    Δύνοντος δὲ τοῦ ἡλίου ἅπαντες ὅσοι εἶχον

ἀσθενοῦντας νόσοις ποικίλαις ἤγαγον αὐτοὺς πρὸς
αὐτόν· ὁ δὲ ἑνὶ ἑκάστῳ αὐτῶν τὰς χεῖρας ἐπιτιθεὶς
ἐθεράπευεν αὐτούς.

15. (Luke 6:28) Bless those who <u>curse</u> you, pray for those who
<u>mistreat</u> you.

εὐλογεῖτε τοὺς καταρωμένους ὑμᾶς, προσεύχεσθε περὶ
τῶν ἐπηρεαζόντων ὑμᾶς.

16

CONDITIONAL SENTENCES:
If I Were You, I Would Read This Chapter

DEVOTIONAL

Matthew 18:30 But he refused. Instead, he went off and had the man thrown into prison until he could pay the debt.

ὁ δὲ οὐκ ἤθελεν ἀλλὰ ἀπελθὼν ἔβαλεν αὐτὸν εἰς φυλακὴν ἕως ἀποδῷ τὸ ὀφειλόμενον.

This passage comes at the end of the parable of the unforgiving servant. The servant had owed a great deal of money. In fact, the ten thousand talents he owed was more than the Roman government possessed at the time. The servant was forgiven of that huge debt, but then he walked out and found another servant who owed him a few dollars.

The parable expects us to believe that the first servant, having been forgiven of so much, will forgive this small debt. The shock comes when the first servant grabs his friend by the throat and has him thrown into debtor's prison.

The king then recalls the first servant and asks about the incident. After learning what has happened, he instructs that the original debt of ten thousand talents be reinstated and has the servant thrown into prison until "he could pay the debt."

This word translated "could pay" is in the subjunctive mood. It indicates that there is some uncertainty as to his ability to repay. In fact, the context indicates that he will never be able to repay such a huge debt. Being thrown into prison "until he could pay" means being thrown into prison forever.

What does Jesus expect us to learn from this story? He expects us to realize that the first servant really didn't understand the wonderful gift offered to him. He expects us to realize that a true experience of forgiveness manifests itself in a willingness to forgive others. When we realize that we have been forgiven of a debt of ten thousand talents against our Lord, a debt that we, like the servant, could never repay, it is then that we become willing to offer personal forgiveness to others around us. Remember that when we pray the Lord's Prayer, we ask the Lord to forgive us as we forgive other people. Do you really want God to use your forgiveness as a standard for his forgiveness of you? If not, perhaps there is someone today whom you need to forgive.

OVERVIEW

The subjunctive mood is a mood of uncertainty. It is the mood of words like "if, might, and could." While the indicative was the mood of certainty (remember that this is a big picture, not every indicative is certain), the subjunctive is a mood of possibility or probability. In the above story there is a possibility that the man could get out of jail, but the context indicates that this possibility is so small as to be almost nonexistent.

Similarities. In English when we wish to express a conditional sentence, we sometimes use the subjunctive in the same way that Greek does. For example, "If I were to pay my debt, I can clear my credit." The condition to clearing the credit is the paying of the debt. In both English and Greek you will often find a sentence using the subjunctive starting with the word "if."

Other uses of the subjunctive use the word "might." This, of course, indicates a certain amount of uncertainty, which usually comes from the first part of the sentence. For example, "I am learning Greek in order that I might read the New Testament." The "might" here indicates uncertainty based on the first part of the sentence. If one does not learn to read Greek, one will never learn to read the New Testament (in Greek at least).

Differences. There are a number of subtle differences between the subjunctive in English and Greek. We will not deal with the minor differences, but four are important. (1) In English with contrary-to-fact conditional statements, we use the subjunctive. For example, "If you had been here, my brother might have lived." In Greek this same sentence would be in the indicative, simply because indirectly a statement of fact has been made; the time of the action has passed and you were not there.

(2) Always think of the Greek subjunctive as a mood of possibility. Whenever the subjunctive is used, there is at least a small nuance of possibility (even though it may be so small as to be almost nonexistent).

(3) A third difference occurs in the first person plural of the subjunctive. There are times when this form of the verb takes on a different task. This is called the hortatory subjunctive* and calls for the translation "let us." In class we call this the sandwich subjunctive because it provides us with the lettuce ("let us"). This form of the verb will not look any different than the regular subjunctive and only the context will help you discover it.

(4) A final difference is that the negation of future actions will often be in the subjunctive. One might read, "When you . . . , don't. . . ." That is, the action that might take place in the future should not be of a kind that is forbidden.

EXERCISES

Circle the subjunctives in the following sentences.

1. I caught a fish in order that we might have supper tonight.

2. If you study this book, you may find Greek a little easier.

3. If you want to improve, you might be thought foolish.

4. Let us begin to worship God.

5. He learned his vocab so that he might guess on the test.

6. (Matthew 6:7) And when you pray, do not keep on babbling like pagans.

   προσευχόμενοι δὲ μὴ βατταλογήσητε ὥσπερ οἱ ἐθνικοί.

7. (Matthew 6:14) For if you forgive men when they sin against you, your heavenly Father will also forgive you.

   ἐὰν γὰρ ἀφῆτε τοῖς ἀνθρώποις τὰ παραπτώματα αὐτῶν, ἀφήσει καὶ ὑμῖν ὁ πατὴρ ὑμῶν ὁ οὐράνιος.

8. (Matthew 8:2) . . . "Lord, if you are willing, you can make me clean."

   Κύριε, ἐὰν θέλῃς δύνασαί με καθαρίσαι.

9. (Matthew 9:6) But so that you may know that the Son of Man has authority on earth to forgive sins. . . .

   ἵνα δὲ εἰδῆτε ὅτι ἐξουσίαν ἔχει ὁ υἱὸς τοῦ ἀνθρώπου ἐπὶ τῆς γῆς ἀφιέναι ἁμαρτίας. . . .

10. (Matthew 15:14) If a blind man leads a blind man, both will fall into a pit.

τυφλὸς δὲ τυφλὸν ἐὰν ὁδηγῇ, ἀμφότεροι εἰς βόθυνον πεσοῦνται.

INFINITIVES:
To Boldly Go Where No Man Has Gone Before: The World's Most Famous Split Infinitive

DEVOTIONAL

Matthew 1:18 This is how the birth of Jesus Christ came about: His mother Mary was pledged to be married to Joseph, but before they <u>came together</u>, she was found to be with child through the Holy Spirit.

Τοῦ δὲ Ἰησοῦ Χριστοῦ ἡ γένεσις οὕτως ἦν. μνηστευθείσης τῆς μητρὸς αὐτοῦ Μαρίας τῷ Ἰωσήφ, πρὶν ἢ <u>συνελθεῖν</u> αὐτοὺς εὑρέθη ἐν γαστρὶ ἔχουσα ἐκ πνεύματος ἁγίου.

Matthew 1:19 Because Joseph her husband was a righteous man and did not want <u>to expose</u> her to public disgrace, he had in mind <u>to divorce</u> her quietly.

Ἰωσὴφ δὲ ὁ ἀνὴρ αὐτῆς, δίκαιος ὢν καὶ μὴ θέλων αὐτὴν <u>δειγματίσαι</u>, ἐβουλήθη λάθρα <u>ἀπολῦσαι</u> αὐτήν.

Matthew 1:20 But after he had considered this, an angel of the Lord appeared to him in a dream and said, "Joseph son of David, do not be afraid <u>to take</u> Mary home as your wife, because what is conceived in her is from the Holy Spirit.

ταῦτα δὲ αὐτοῦ ἐνθυμηθέντος ἰδοὺ ἄγγελος κυρίου κατ᾽ ὄναρ ἐφάνη αὐτῷ λέγων, Ἰωσὴφ υἱὸς Δαυίδ, μὴ φοβηθῇς <u>παραλαβεῖν</u> Μαριὰμ τὴν γυναῖκά σου, τὸ γὰρ ἐν αὐτῇ γεννηθὲν ἐκ πνεύματός ἐστιν ἁγίου.

We have all, at one time or another, found ourselves in the shoes of Job of the Hebrew Bible. We ask God "Why?" when we face a particular difficulty.

Joseph in Matthew 1 finds himself in a troublesome situation. He is confused by the fact that his beloved finacée has become pregnant. A glance at the Greek infinitives of this story will help us to understand what Joseph was going through.

In Matthew 1:18, Joseph and Mary are about "to come together" and Mary is found to be pregnant. One can imagine the thoughts that must have run through the head of Joseph (who interestingly, never speaks in the Scripture). He is surprised and hurt.

This hurt leads to two more infinitives, which occur when Joseph decides "to put [Mary] away" quietly. Despite his disappointment, he still wants to treat Mary with respect and kindness. Rather than subject her to public humiliation, he decides not to expose her but to let her go away in silence.

At that point an angel appears to Joseph (not the only time an angel appears with valuable information for Joseph; see 2:13) and tells him that the child is from the Holy Spirit. The angel also gives Joseph an infinitive when he tells Joseph not to be afraid "to take" this woman as his wife. Joseph listens to the angel and in an incredible act of faith and grace takes Mary despite all outward indications. This infinitive reminds us that God works in ways that we could never expect or even comprehend. When you face the difficulties of a tiring semester, don't hesitate to turn back to these infinitives that brought Joseph hope in the midst of difficulty.

There will, no doubt, be times when you wonder how God is going to work everything out for his glory. Remember the infinitives of Joseph and the wonderful story of redemption that came about because he obeyed the Lord in difficult times.

INTRODUCTION

Many of you can reach back into the deep recesses of your grammar or high school education and remember a teacher who said to you, "Do not split infinitives." At the time (and perhaps even today) you may not have been sure of what he was talking about. While we may not remember our grammar, virtually all of us remember the great opening line from the *Star Trek* series: "To boldly go where no man has gone before." The problem is that if this phrase had appeared on a seventh grade literature paper, it would have been marked off for being a "split infinitive." An infinitive is a verb that begins with "to . . ."; for example, "to turn," "to go," "to see" are all infinitives. The English grammar rule (which has been relaxed some since our days in school) stated that there should be nothing between the "to" and the verb. Thus "to boldly go" was a split infinitive because it placed "boldly" between "to" and "go."

In Greek it is impossible to split an infinitive because it is one word, not two. Just as in English, the Greek infinitive can have a variety of uses, such as purpose (He went to the store in order to get milk) and result (He went to jail after failing to rob the bank).

DEFINITION

While the participle is a verbal adjective, the infinitive is a verbal noun. The verb is called an infinitive because of the fact that it is not time bound; thus it is (in some sense) infinite. Because of this, the infinitive will almost always be used with a finite verb* (one bound by time). An example of this would be, "The man walked in order to lose weight." The time aspect of the sentence is found in the finite verb* ("walked"), not in the infinitive ("to lose"). To change the idea to the future time, the infinitive does not need to be changed, only the finite verb: "The man will walk in order to lose weight."

The noun portion of the infinitive stems from the fact that often the infinitive will function as a substantive* in the sentence (e.g., "To see is to believe"). While functioning as a substantive, often the infinitive will have verbal qualities. Thus it is a verbal noun.

Differences. One of the main differences between the Greek and English infinitive, as already noted, is that the Greek infinitive is only one word and is thus impossible to "split."

A second and perhaps more important difference is that the Greek infinitive, as a verbal noun, will sometimes have an article. In years to come you will learn from your grammar that the use of the article can be very important in understanding the infinitive.

A third difference is that the infinitive in Greek will often be placed together with certain cases of the article or certain prepositions in order to make clear the particular usage of the infinitive in the sentence. You will see these uses in overview in the first-year grammar and in more detail as you study the language more carefully.

EXERCISES

Circle the infinitive in the following sentences.

1. The best students formed a study group in order to raise their grades.

2. I went to the store so that I could get the milk needed to make the cake.

3. To many people, the study of Greek is of little value when one wants to get a job.

4. (1 Corinthians 1:17) For Christ did not send me to baptize, but to preach the gospel.

   οὐ γὰρ ἀπέστειλέν με Χριστὸς βαπτίζειν ἀλλὰ εὐαγγελίζεσθαι.

5. (1 Corinthians 1:21) God was pleased through the foolishness of what was preached to save those who believe.

   εὐδόκησεν ὁ θεὸς διὰ τῆς μωρίας τοῦ κηρύγματος σῶσαι τοὺς πιστεύοντας.

6. (1 Corinthians 5:9) I have written you in my letter not to associate with sexually immoral people.

   Ἔγραψα ὑμῖν ἐν τῇ ἐπιστολῇ μὴ συναναμίγνυσθαι πόρνοις.

7. (1 Corinthians 9:4) Don't we have the right to food and drink?

   μὴ οὐκ ἔχομεν ἐξουσίαν φαγεῖν καὶ πεῖν;

8. (2 Corinthians 1:15) Because I was confident of this, I planned to visit you first so that you might benefit twice.

Καὶ ταύτῃ τῇ πεποιθήσει ἐβουλόμην πρότερον πρὸς ὑμᾶς ἐλθεῖν, ἵνα δευτέραν χάριν σχῆτε.

9. (2 Corinthians 10:6) And we will be ready to punish every act of disobedience, once your obedience is complete.

καὶ ἐν ἑτοίμῳ ἔχοντες ἐκδικῆσαι πᾶσαν παρακοήν, ὅταν πληρωθῇ ὑμῶν ἡ ὑπακοή.

10. (2 Corinthians 12:4) He heard inexpressible things, things that man is not permitted to tell.

ἤκουσεν ἄρρητα ῥήματα ἃ οὐκ ἐξὸν ἀνθρώπῳ λαλῆσαι.

18

IMPERATIVES:
Read This Chapter!
The Bosses of the Greek World

DEVOTIONAL

Matthew 27:22 "What shall I do, then, with Jesus who is called Christ?" Pilate asked. They all answered, "Crucify him!"

λέγει αὐτοῖς ὁ Πιλᾶτος, Τί οὖν ποιήσω Ἰησοῦν τὸν λεγόμενον Χριστόν; λέγουσιν πάντες, Σταυρωθήτω.

As I write this, the film *The Passion of the Christ* is about to be released amidst a great deal of controversy. There are those who say that the movie will engender a new wave of anti-Semitism in our country and perhaps the world. After all, Matthew has the Jews crying out for the crucifixion of Jesus and asking for his blood to be on them and on their children. Isn't this a direct claim that the Jewish people of Jesus day were responsible for his crucifixion?

The question of "Who crucified Jesus?" is a large one. The short answer is that we all did. We all carry around the nails in our pockets with which Jesus was crucified. If we had been there that day, we might have found ourselves shouting for his crucifixion.

We should notice that the cry "Crucify him!" is in the imperative mood. Notice also that some other versions translate the cry of the Jews differently from the way that the phrase is translated in the NIV. The reason for this is that the Greek word used here is a third person imperative (which we do not have in English), a distinction that will be explained more carefully below.

In the end, the ultimate answer to the question of the person or group who crucified Jesus must be met with what may seem to be a counter-intuitive answer. God the Father crucified Jesus. The redemption of the human race was a part of the great plan of our gracious Father. While our sin is responsible for the crucifixion, God's good providence is also responsible. Let us never forget that God planned before the foundation of the world to bring about our salvation through the death of our Lord and Savior Jesus Christ.

OVERVIEW

Remember when you were in first grade that there was one student (there is one in every class) who took great pleasure in bossing everyone around? No matter what happened, this student had a better way of doing things and had to tell everyone how and why they should be acting in a particular way.

The imperative is the Greek version of that student. It is the grammatical form that takes pleasure in bossing everyone around. Sometimes the bossing is very aggressive (an imperative of command), at other times it is more of a suggestion (imperative of entreaty). Never forget, however, that the imperative is the boss of the Greek world.

Similarities. There are many similarities between the Greek and English imperatives. (1) They both are moods* of command. They command, ask, or advise the hearer to do something. (2) This is one of the rare cases in English where the subject can be contained in the verb, as is always the case in Greek. The sentence

"Shut the book!" has as its subject the word "you," since you are being commanded to close the book. Yet the word "you" does not occur in the sentence. As you may remember from fifth grade grammar class, the "you" is the implied subject of the sentence.

Differences. Despite the similarities, there are differences between the Greek and English imperatives. The most important and most difficult of these differences is the fact that there is a third person imperative in Greek. Remember in English that the implied subject is *always* "you" (singular or plural). No matter what the command was, it always comes to "you."

In Greek, one is not only able to command a person to whom you are speaking (i.e., like the English imperative), but also a person about whom you are speaking. This is what leads to the difference in translation in the above passage of Scripture. The NIV translates this passage as if it were a second person imperative (a perfectly allowable translation choice): "Crucify him!" In reality, however, the word is a third person imperative and thus can be translated, "Let him be crucified." The difference is in the subject of the verb. The second person has as its subject Pilate, the third person has its subject Jesus.

This difference between first and second person is often difficult for students to grasp hold of. Simply remember that the command to a person with whom you are speaking is a direct command, and a command about another person to whom you are not speaking is a more distant command, which is usually translated "let him/her be. . . ."

EXERCISES

Circle each of the imperatives.

1.   Please get up and close the door.

2. Turn off the light before you leave.

3. Study hard for the upcoming test.

4. Don't think that you do not need to review your vocabulary.

5. Stop talking and listen.

6. (2 Timothy 1:13) What you heard from me, keep as the pattern of sound teaching, with faith and love in Christ Jesus.

   ὑποτύπωσιν ἔχε ὑγιαινόντων λόγων ὧν παρ᾽ ἐμοῦ ἤκουσας ἐν πίστει καὶ ἀγάπῃ τῇ ἐν Χριστῷ Ἰησοῦ.

7. (2 Timothy 2:1) You then, my son, be strong in the grace that is in Christ Jesus.

   Σὺ οὖν, τέκνον μου, ἐνδυναμοῦ ἐν τῇ χάριτι τῇ ἐυ Χριστῷ Ἰησοῦ.

8. (Mark 15:32) Let Christ the King of Israel descend now from the cross, that we may see and believe.

   ὁ Χριστὸς ὁ βασιλεὺς Ἰσραὴλ καταβάτω νῦν ἀπὸ τοῦ σταυροῦ, ἵνα ἴδωμεν καὶ πιστεύσωμεν.

9. (Luke 8:8) When he said this, he called out, "He who has ears to hear, let him hear."

   ὁ ἔχων ὦτα ἀκούειν ἀκουέτω.

10. (1 Corinthians 7:11) But if she does, she must remain unmarried . . . .

    ἐὰν δὲ καὶ χωρισθῇ, μενέτω ἄγαμος.

APPENDIX 1: GLOSSARY OF TERMS

active One of three voices used by verbs. It indicates that the subject is doing the action. See also *middle* and *passive*. See chapter 6 and *BBG*, p. 124.

adjective A word used to describe a noun or to stand for a noun or substantive. This word will usually tell something about the noun (e.g., the *blue* hair). See chapter 4 and *BBG* chapter 9.

adverb A word that describes a verb or tells how the action was accomplished (e.g., "the man was running *fast*).

anarthrous Without the article. Any word in Greek that does not have the definite article is said to be anarthrous.

aorist One of the tenses of the verb. This tense may indicate past action but can also be seen as simply the default tense. See chapter 13 and *BBG* chapter 22.

article In English there are both definite and indefinite articles ("the" as opposed to "a/an"). In Greek there is no indefinite article, only the definite article. This article, meaning "the" (there are other uses that you will learn later), is helpful in many other ways in the study of Greek. See chapter 3 and *BBG* chapter 7.

articular Having the article. See also *article* and *anarthrous*.

attributive Describes a part of speech (usually an adjective) that directly modifies a substantive. See also *adjective* and *substantive*. See *BBG*, pp. 65–66.

augment   A vowel that occurs at the start of a verb to indicate both indicative mood and past tense. In Greek, one will only find the augment in the imperfect or the aorist tense. See *BBG*, pp. 184–85. (Note that it also occurs in the pluperfect, but this form is so rare that it has been excluded.)

case   Greek, being an inflected language, uses a particular spelling of the word (a case) to indicate the function in a sentence. The cases are explained in chapter 2.

clause   A construction that is in some sense grammatically complete. There are two kinds of clauses in Greek: dependent (dependent on some other clause in the sentence); independent (not dependent on some other clause). The clause will contain some verbal form.

conditional   A construction in which the action predicted by a
future   future verb is conditioned on some action that may or may not take place. "If you study, you will do well."

contract verb A verb whose stem ends in vowel. This causes a contraction between the connecting vowel and the stem vowel (not in all tenses), which will often cause the verb to look slightly odd. If one learns the true endings, the contract verbs will cause no problem. See chapter 8 and *BBG* chapter 17.

declension   A way of spelling a noun or substantive to indicate the word's use in the sentence. For example, a word spelled in the nominative will be the subject. There are three declensions in Greek, but all of them denote simply a difference in spelling, not in meaning. That is, a nominative in the second declension is grammatically no different from a nominative in the first. See chapter 2 and *BBG*, pp. 29–32.

direct object The object on which the subject of the sentence is acting. See chapters 1 and 2.

divine passive A verb used in the passive voice for the express purpose of not naming God as the subject. "Blessed is he who . . ." is an example of a divine passive. God blesses, but his name is not used.

finite verb Any verb that has "person." For example, an infinitive does not have person and thus is not a finite verb. Any verb about which you can say X person (singular or plural) will be a finite verb. See also *person*.

future A tense that (often) points toward an action that has not yet happened. See chapter 11 and *BBG* chapter 19.

gender The component of a word that identifies the term as either masculine, feminine, or neuter. Keep in mind that a word's gender will often not translate into English (e.g., we do not call truth "she").

imperative A verbal use (mood) that indicates some sort of command or entreaty. See also mood and *BBG* chapter 33.

imperfect A tense that indicates an ongoing action, often (particularly in the indicative) in the past. It differs from the aorist in that the action is ongoing. See *BBG* chapter 22.

indicative A verbal mood that often indicates certainty (on the part of the speaker) of action.

infinitive A verbal use in which the verb has no person or number; thus the verb is "infinite." It is often translated "to . . ." rather than "I (or you or he/she/it). . . ." See chapter 15 and *BBG* chapter 32.

inflected   A language that indicates parts of speech by different spellings rather than by the word's placement in the sentence. See chapter 2.

lexical form   The Greek/English dictionary is called a "lexicon." The lexical form is the spelling of the word that one will find listed in the lexicon. For nouns it is the nominative singular; for verbs it is the first person singular (usually present indicative).

middle voice   The middle voice was passing out of use during the time of the writing of the New Testament; thus there are not many "true" middle usages found in the text. A true middle will often indicate that the action of the verb has in some way affected the subject.

mood   This is the part of the Greek verbal system that indicates the nature of the verb and how it relates to reality. For example, the indicative is the mood that presents the verbal activity as being actual, while the subjunctive presents it as only being possible.

morphology   The study of the system of words. Morphological questions ask why a certain word has changed in a certain manner. See Mounce's *The Morphology of Biblical Greek*.

noun   A person, place, thing, or idea. See chapter 1 or *BBG* chapter 5.

number   In substantives as well as verbs, the number will be either singular or plural. The number of a verb will agree with its subject.

participle   A participle is a verbal adjective. As such it can both act as an adjective (with the qualities of a substantive) and as a verb (with the qualities of a verb). Participles are declined like adjectives. See chapter 15 or *BBG* chapter 26.

passive voice　A verb in which the subject is being acted upon rather than doing the action. For example: "John was hit by the ball" (the ball is acting on John rather than John on the ball). See chapter 9 or *BBG* chapter 18. See also *divine passive*.

person　All finite verbs will be first, second, or third person. First person is "I" or "we"; second person is "you"; third person is "he/she/it" or "they." See chapter 6 or *BBG* chapter 15.

predicate　A part of the sentence that includes the verb and often something about the subject. Thus there is something being "predicated" about the subject.

principal part　All verbs have six potential principal parts. When a verb changes tense (e.g., from present to aorist), its principal parts changes. Not all verbs will have all six principal parts; some are only used in the New Testament in a few tenses rather than all. Note that Mounce in *BBG* calls these "tense stems," but most other grammars will call them principal parts. In his verb charts, Mounce draws a line in place of a word where a particular verb does not have a principal part reflected in the New Testament. See chapter 12 or *BBG* chapter 20.

pronoun　A substantive that takes the place of a noun (personal pronouns are "I, you, he, she," etc.). A pronoun must agree in gender and number with the noun it is modifying. See chapter 5 or *BBG* chapter 11.

source The lexical form of a word. Usually this will be the particular form of the word that you learned as a vocabulary word. In nouns it is the nominative singular; in verbs, the first person singular.

subject The most important noun in the sentence. When an active verb is used, the subject will perform the action. When a passive verb is used, the subject will receive the action.

subjunctive A mood of the Greek verb that deals with possibility. The subjunctive mood sees the action of the verb as possible or probable.

substantive A noun or any other word (e.g., a participle) that functions like a noun. Any word that acts as a person, place, thing, or idea is a candidate for being a substantive. Think of it as a substitute teacher that is doing the job of the real teacher.

syntax The study of how words are put together to make a clause, phrase, or sentence. This includes the study of different uses of particular cases, moods, tenses, and so on.

tense This is the part of the verb that indicates either aspect or time. For example, the imperfect indicates continuing action. There is some debate today about how much the tense of a verb indicates about time. See chapter 6 and *BBG* chapter 15.

verb There must be a verb in every sentence (either stated or implied). It indicates either an action or a state of being.

voice All verbs and verbals will have one of three voices. In the active voice the subject is doing the action. About the middle voice there is much debate, but one can usually see some sort of reflexive action in which the subject is doing something to or for itself. In the passive voice the subject is being acted upon.

word order   The meaning and function of a word in a sentence is decided in English by word order. For example, the general word order for an English sentence is subject, verb, object. Because Greek is an inflected language, word order plays a much smaller role in establishing meaning.

APPENDIX 2:
TIPS FOR REMEMBERING
VOCABULARY

Recent study has shown that knowing vocabulary may be the most important part of learning a language. Of course the study of grammar is critically important, but all the grammatical knowledge in the world will be of little use if you do not know what the words mean. So here are a few tips that may help with learning vocabulary in any language.

Flash cards. Make or buy them and keep them with you at all times. Review them right before going to sleep. If you are using Mounce's text, you will be able to take the vocabulary list from the CD-ROM and print it out. The list should include the part of speech as well as the chapter, so that you can review chapter by chapter. The only difficulty is that you should be careful about reviewing words in the same order all the time. You may fool yourself into thinking that you know more than you do. This same problem manifests itself in homemade vocabulary cards. Your handwriting, small stains on the card, and so on, may give you subtle clues that will not occur on the test. Thus you need some method for mixing up the cards into a random order. This will not be possible if the words are printed out on a few sheets of paper, but the vocabulary program that comes with Mounce's grammar will be very helpful here.

Computer programs. If you are using Mounce's textbook, the much improved second edition of the CD-ROM will be of invaluable assistance here. If you are using another text, you might consider Greek Flash Pro 2.0 CD-ROM from Paradigm Software.

Mnemonic association. This technique is perhaps the most important and helpful tool for vocabulary memorization. In short, the idea is to associate that which you do not know with that which you do know. The key is to make a mental picture that includes both the familiar (what you do know) and the unfamiliar (the new word). Do all that you can to make these associations into mental pictures that are clear and easy to remember. In order to accomplish this the associations should be:

☞ larger than life

☞ moving (i.e., animated)

☞ painful or funny

An example of this technique can be seen in the memorization of the Greek word ἁμαρτόλος (*hamartolos*). The word sounds like the word "hammer toe loss" and means a sinner or sin. Think of a person with a very large hammer (larger than life), who is using that tool (movement) to hammer your toes (painful). He hammers so hard that you lose a toe and thus you end up with "hammer toe loss." You should have no trouble remembering that to hammer your toe so hard that you lose it would be a sin, and thus this word will stick with you.

Remember that the mind is looking for "hooks" to hang new ideas or words on. If you can make those hooks words or (preferably) pictures that you already know, the association will stand you in good stead when it comes time for a vocabulary test.

APPENDIX 3:
SENTENCE DIAGRAMMING
FOR GREEK FUN AND PROFIT

At some point in your distant past, you had a teacher who trained you to diagram sentences. This was to help you visualize each part of speech and remember what role it played in the drama of the sentence. Diagramming Greek sentences can be just as helpful. There are a few rules that will be of great benefit to you as you begin your journey in translating sentences. You must break up the sentence into clauses (often punctuation will help); then apply these rules.

1. *Always start by finding the verb.* Place the main verb on the base line in the middle (see example). This is particularly important, given the fact that the subject in Greek will not always be stated (that is, it will sometimes be contained inside the verb).

2. *Look for the subject.* Place the subject on the base line in front of the verb. It is important to note that a first or second person verb will only have a pronoun for a subject and will be for emphasis. Any verb that has a proper noun for a subject must be in the third person.

3. *Look for the object.* What is the subject doing with the verb, and to whom or what is she doing it? Place the object on the base line after the verb.

If you will look for these three things, the rest of the phrase will become easy. The value of diagramming these phrases for the first few weeks is that it trains your mind to look for the proper parts of speech in the proper order, and it gives you a visual picture of how the phrase or sentence fits together. What follows is a diagram to get you started. It was made using the diagramming tool found (along with many other very valuable tools) in Bible-Works 6.

Sentence: The girl drove the car.

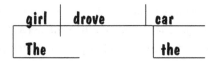

Notice that the verb, subject, and object are all on one base line. The subject comes first, the verb after, and the object after the verb. The articles tell us something about the noun and are thus placed under the nouns. Drawing a base line and finding the verb, subject, and object will go a long way in helping you in your efforts to understand the inflected nature of Greek.

We want to hear from you. Please send your comments about
this book to us in care of zreview@zondervan.com. Thank you.